T0008230

"Incorporating guidance from therapists a[nd] Harts takes a comprehensive look at what [racial] trauma can look like and provides strategies for how to talk about it. Moving beyond how to heal, Harts also points toward the future and shares tactics to help women of color succeed in their workplaces."
—*TIME*, "8 New Books You Should Read in October"

"Recovering from racial trauma is a radical act and a labor of love. In an act of brave vulnerability, Harts explains step-by-step how she healed, and how you can too. If you want to be a better champion for your colleagues who have experienced racism at work, or a boss who creates a work environment that heals rather than retraumatizing your employees, this is the book you need to read. Now."
—Kim Scott, *New York Times*–bestselling author of *Radical Candor*

"With care, conviction, and deep insight, Harts instructs us on how to heal from racial trauma at work. Onward to healing."
—Ibram X. Kendi

"Harts's new book, *Right Within*, is one I'm taking my time to read—its purpose is to help women of colour heal from racial trauma in the workplace, and Harts absolutely delivers on that."
—Priyanka Khanna, *Vogue India*

"Being invited to the table is not the same as being welcomed and valued at the table, which is what women of color continue to aspire to in the workplace. *Right Within* compels women of color across generations to address racialized trauma by speaking up, healing from within, and identifying triggers. You will benefit greatly from reading it and putting its wisdom into practice."

—Melonie Parker, chief diversity officer, Google

"Harts argues that we need to understand that racism kills both people and careers, and that workplace injustices do incredible harm. She goes on to explain the labor involved with being the only Black woman in the office, facing microaggressions from colleagues and a lack of support from human resources. This vital guidebook for women of color in the workplace urges readers to understand there are paths forward, and to remember that they are not alone."

—*Booklist*

"A moving guide to healing and equity. Harts is a voice to be reckoned with. Everyone needs to read this book."

—LaTosha Brown, cofounder of Black Voters Matter

"Harts offers advice on how women can acknowledge their pain and recover from their heartbreaks with the right healing tools, and she continues to raise awareness about these challenges among industry leaders and managers."

—*Entrepreneur*

"Harts highlights that what matters most is valuing you, and trusting yourself enough to push through obstacles faced on a daily basis. A powerful, necessary read for women of color—and everyone—seeking to tap into their resilience from within."

—Barbara Whye, VP of diversity and inclusion, Apple

"A frank-talking field guide for 'how to deal with microaggressions, heal from racialized trauma, and find relief from invisible workplace burdens.' Most importantly, it includes insights on how to advocate for oneself and an equitable, inclusive workplace, even when on unequal footing."

—*The Root*

"Harts puts so much that needs to be said into words, and her advice is priceless. This is the guide we've been waiting for."

—La La Anthony, TV producer, actress, and author of
The Love Playbook

"With resilience and self-preservation, Harts guides the reader through her personal journey, providing expert advice on how we, too, can overcome and heal from ongoing racial discrimination."

—Dr. Sheila Robinson, publisher & CEO, Diversity
Woman Media

Right Within

HOW TO HEAL FROM RACIAL TRAUMA IN THE WORKPLACE

MINDA HARTS

SEAL PRESS

New York

*Dedicated to all the Black women who
were told they had to be strong for someone
else, instead of for themselves.*

Seal Press
Hachette Book Group
1290 Avenue of the Americas, New York, NY 10104
www.sealpress.com
@sealpress

Printed in the United States of America

Originally published in hardcover and ebook by Seal Press in October 2021
First Trade Paperback Edition: October 2022

Published by Seal Press, an imprint of Perseus Books, LLC, a subsidiary of Hachette Book Group, Inc. The Seal Press name and logo is a trademark of the Hachette Book Group.

The Hachette Speakers Bureau provides a wide range of authors for speaking events. To find out more, go to www.hachettespeakersbureau.com or call (866) 376-6591.

The publisher is not responsible for websites (or their content) that are not owned by the publisher.

Print book interior design by Trish Wilkinson.

Library of Congress Cataloging-in-Publication Data
Names: Harts, Minda, author.
Title: Right within: how to heal from racial trauma in the workplace / Minda Harts.
Description: New York: Seal Press, 2021. | Includes index. |
Identifiers: LCCN 2021022124 | ISBN 9781541619623 (hardcover) | ISBN 9781541619630 (ebook)
Subjects: LCSH: Diversity in the workplace. | Minority women—Employment. | Microaggressions.
Classification: LCC HF5549.5.M5 H3687 2021 | DDC 658.3008—dc23
LC record available at https://lccn.loc.gov/2021022124

ISBNs: 9781541619623 (hardcover); 9781541619630 (ebook); 9781541619647 (trade paperback)

LSC-C

Printing 1, 2022

CONTENTS

I think we need people with courage and vision.

—Octavia E. Butler

AUTHOR'S NOTE

I chose to change some identifying details such as locations, companies, organizations, occupations, and names of those I worked with in the past. I consciously made the decision to maintain their anonymity. I have recalled my racially charged experiences in the workplace and conversations based on my memory of them. Additionally, the stories that I share from other women of color about their workplace experiences—their stories are told based on their perception and/or experiences related to the inequality they faced. All the resources shared in this book are only recommendations; so please, do your own research and due diligence if you decide to use them going forward.

PREFACE

How would I describe my life in the year 2020 in just one word? I would probably say stressed. As a Black woman who spent the majority of that year inside my apartment due to the pandemic, stressed might not even begin to fully capture my emotional state. I guess you could say that in addition to feeling *stressed* because I didn't want to catch the coronavirus, I was also *exhausted* due to the racism on full display from the highest office in this country, the presidency.

Oh come on, don't act like you forgot how crazy 2020 was. Masks, hand sanitizer, and bleach were hard to come by. It was also a huge election year, and many of us were feeling like our backs were against the wall. I felt like the Chicago rap group Do or Die: I was willing to ride in the back seat of any Caddy if it meant I would never have to see Donald in that office ever again. I had so many conversations with friends about what options were available to us if Trump got another four years in office. We were legit nervous, anxious, and downright scared of where things were headed for minorities

1

in our country. I had never felt worried about being a Black woman in this country until 2020.

I remember going on long strolls with my mask on around the nearby pond, but toward the end of that year, I avoided unnecessary walks because I feared being attacked or verbally assaulted. I still would walk my dog, but whenever I saw a pickup truck, I immediately felt triggered because I thought about Ahmaud Arbery. He was just out for a jog and then was gunned down by three white men in a pickup truck in Georgia. Some might say, *That is ludicrous, Minda*, but that is how I felt, and as much as I didn't want to feel that way, my fear was real for me. My uncle in my head, the late James Baldwin, said, "I love America more than any other country in the world and, exactly for this reason, I insist on the right to criticize her perpetually." I felt this same conflicted love for the only country I have ever lived in, and all I wanted was for it to love my people back. Was that too much to ask?

I began to understand why people like Marcus Garvey felt the need to return to Africa. But I also connected with Angela Davis's work: she wanted to stay and fight to dismantle a system that has never worked for us, and fight for the generations who haven't yet been born. I grappled heavily with the trauma I felt when Trayvon Martin's young life was brutally taken from him, and in 2020 I felt that pain all over again with the deaths of Breonna Taylor and George Floyd. So I guess we can add a third word to describe my feelings in 2020: *triggered*.

What more can we do, how many more marches do we need to have, to convince folks that Black Lives Matter? I felt triggered by all the racial unrest. I started to thank God that at that time in my life I didn't have a traditional job in corporate America, because I don't think I could have shown up in a virtual environment and pretended like everything was business as usual. Nor could I work for a company that still refused to even state publicly that my life mattered. I woke up every morning and said a little prayer for my sisters who had struggled the night before and then had to deal with a sea of white faces on Zoom or Google Hangouts and pretend that this sh*t didn't weigh them down like a ton of Hefty garbage bags.

If you were a white person during this hectic year, I am sure you also felt the upheaval. But you never had to worry about having "the talk" with your Black son, nor did you have to worry that your Black daughter might be gunned down in her apartment while hanging out with the love of her life. Black and Brown folks don't get the benefit of turning off the television when we've had too much of a certain news story—we are still Black and Brown when everyone else goes to bed.

And then, on top of everything, in 2020 I had the privilege of writing my next book, *Right Within*, the one you are reading or listening to right now. A book about how we heal from racialized work trauma. A book I was so excited to write for us, a book that I am still excited for you to read. But I have to be honest with you, the experience of writing this book was much different than the experience of writing my first book, *The Memo: What Women of Color Need to Know to Secure a Seat at the Table*. I struggled writing this book, because I was also in a state of racialized trauma from the overlapping crises of 2020. What our country was going through—hell, what

Black people were experiencing in 2020—started to flood my mind, and at the same time I was overwhelmed working through all of my experiences from previous years inside and outside of the workplace. I couldn't stop thinking about Breonna Taylor, Sandra Bland, and Cynthia Hurd.

Breonna Taylor, Sandra Bland, and Cynthia Hurd had a few things in common. They were all Black women, they all died due to systemic racism, and they were all Black women in the workplace. It has been said that Breonna Taylor had sticky notes around her apartment with the goals she planned to accomplish that year and in the years to come. I don't know about you, but I have sticky notes all over my office with some of the same goals. I began to think about these women, their dreams, their goals, and even their fears. In those moments, I realized that racism doesn't just kill people, it kills careers too. Breonna and Cynthia each had a career, while Sandra was about to start a new one. And just to be clear, I am not equating murder with the racial assaults that happen inside the workplace; what I am saying is workplace injustices hurt too. It is damaging to know that if you had been a different color, your life or career might have mattered more.

I began to think about the many times racism tried to kill my career, and how heavy I felt during those times in my life. The times when I wasn't sure I could make it through the workday because a manager said something racially inappropriate, but I was the one who supposedly "took it the wrong way." I mean, what other way am I supposed to take comments that start with "You people"? After building my career for over fifteen years, there were days when I wasn't sure how much longer I would be able to last being the only

Black woman in the office. Being the "only" is more emotionally taxing than the dominant majority will ever know. And eventually, it leaves many of us not feeling right within. This led me to start to investigate the importance of being right within and learning how to pack a little lighter. Too often, workplace burdens will other you in some way, shape, or form. And while you can't control everything, you can center yourself and find ways to heal.

Even in those moments when I felt like crying and throwing the covers over my head because I was so overwhelmed by the trauma all around me, I started to find some joy in exploring what healing could look like for women of color. I started to explore the consequences of not taking time to heal from racialized trauma. Many of us have experienced so much of this trauma in the workplace that, in order to function, we desperately needed to lock away and forget those memories. And some of us are reminded of that trauma every day, because we work in an environment that won't allow us to live our best lives. You know, those environments that extend more grace to the person doing the harm than to the person who was harmed. The reason for healing and becoming right within is not to benefit corporate America, academia, or your nonprofit organization—healing is for us.

Some of our electronic purchases first require we get a double-A battery, or the fine print might say, "Assembly required." Well, if you have spent any time in the workplace as a woman of color, then healing will be required if you want to secure your seat at the table. You might be thinking, *What table and what seat are you referring to, Minda?* Having a seat at the table means that you are part of the decision-making process or you have influence within your workplace. You are valued and you have leaders who are invested in your career success. Often we are experiencing our racialized trauma in isolation and struggling to make some sense of it all. But we have the power to free ourselves from the stranglehold of workplace racial trauma. It's not an easy feat, and, let's be honest, some of us haven't even considered what healing might look like when it comes to what Jim said to us ten years ago. Or how something Karen said last week might affect how we show up in other spaces. Lauryn Hill asked us a very timely, and timeless, question circa 1998: "How you gonna win, when you ain't right within?" We need to investigate and interrogate how to be free from all of those racialized aggressions. Pushing away the pain, rather than confronting it and healing, only hurts us in the end, stunting our personal and professional growth.

Before I wrote *Right Within*, I thought I had healed from many of my workplace traumas (praise the Lord). But as I began to write this book, I discovered there were places in my career journey that I had to revisit, and I finally came face-to-face with the pain others had inflicted upon me. I thought that I had to rationalize away those experiences, that that was the only way I could make it through a workweek and not completely break down. I didn't realize how many racialized experiences I had suppressed. Through my own investigative work, I needed to address all of them, because the pain was affecting other areas of my life. And I don't have to be a therapist to know that unresolved trauma doesn't serve me, or anyone.

So I ask you to take a ride with me to explore what healing from racialized workplace trauma might look like for you. And, more importantly, what freedom could feel like. Healing can be messy, it can be complicated, but I am here to be your guide, your sista friend, and your mentor as we uncover a freedom that the women who came before us never experienced. We have the unique opportunity and privilege to choose a path toward healing. We owe this to ourselves and to future generations of women of color, who need to know that healing is possible for them too. Shall we begin?

Chapter 1

I CAN'T GIVE UP NOW

Nobody told me
The road would be easy
—Mary Mary, "Can't Give Up Now"

I have always been the only Black woman in the room. Meaning, in the course of my career, I was the only Black woman in the boardroom and the only Black woman in the break room. And I hate to admit to you that, at times, it was a lonely journey. I've eaten way too many lunches alone. I started to settle into the microaggressions and the bias that so effortlessly tended to greet me at any given time during the workday. I don't know how many times I've told myself that Bob didn't mean any harm, and neither did Kim. Maybe you have created the same fairy tale so that you could get through your workday too. The crazy thing about this narrative is that I began to believe it. In my previous career, I started to feed myself tablespoons of BS—little by little, over fifteen years— and none of that brought me any peace. It only resulted in me questioning my self-worth.

I spent a lot of time questioning. Questioning if what I was experiencing at work was in fact racism, or if I was just reading too much into the situation. I would question if my colleague was just being a jerk or if they were being ignorant. All of that led to even more questioning, especially toward myself. I believe systemic racism was created to make people of color question themselves.

Now, before you go any further in this book, one thing you should know about me from the jump is that I am going to keep it real with you. If I am going to get vulnerable with you about my journey toward healing from toxic workplaces, in return, I hope you're willing to be vulnerable and unpack your racialized baggage along with me, so that you can be right within.

Please don't pretend that you forgot the famous song "Bag Lady" by Erykah Badu: "One day all them bags gon' get in your way, so pack light." I realize this song might not be talking exclusively about racialized work trauma, but Ms. Badu wasn't wrong. I don't know about you, but there was a time in my not-so-distant past when I had all kinds of workplace trauma in my bags. And to be very clear, my trauma wasn't tucked inside a fancy designer handbag. My baggage was so battered and strained, it started to look like those cheap plastic grocery bags, about to rip open at any moment. When we don't know what to do with those burdens, we sometimes try to deny they exist, only making matters worse.

Recently, I was on a panel with the CEO of DiversityInc, Carolynn Johnson, and she said she didn't believe in unconscious bias, but she believed in unchecked bias. I wanted to throw my invisible church fan in the air when she made that comment. For so many years, we have made excuses for many of our white colleagues' unchecked racialized behavior in the workplace. And because many of us don't have the agency at work to speak truth to power without facing backlash, we try to pretend we aren't hurt and tell ourselves that our colleagues had no ill intent. I often think about an old manager who constantly made racialized comments to me about my hair or the bright colors I wore. Those comments always ended with him making jokes at my expense. And even though I unfortunately had learned to laugh through the pain, it didn't make his words hurt any less. They just added another invisible cut, and my white counterparts never had the emotional intelligence to see my racialized scars. With each racialized experience, it was like salt being poured on reopened wounds, and there is no Band-Aid big enough to heal the pain. The last time I checked, dealing with racialized work trauma was not in the job description. I think I might need some workers' compensation, because these darn racialized trauma bags are causing me some severe back pain. And since you are reading or listening to this book, I hope you are ready to lighten a load that you should never have been burdened with in the first place.

MY THESIS

I began to realize that women of color needed to solve a big problem. The problem is that many of us have never given ourselves permission to address and heal from the trauma we've encountered from oppressive workplaces. The older tools of denial don't work; they just enable the gaslighting to continue. The burden shouldn't be ours to carry, but we can help each other tell the truth, validate our experiences, and let go of what we can. We can give ourselves space to reaffirm our value first to ourselves, and then to everyone in the boardroom. We need to breathe easier so we can take our rightful place at the table. We deserve to be right within.

Most of us have been suffering in silence, sweeping our trauma under the rug, or pretending those workplace devastations didn't affect us. You know those times your manager told you that you weren't "ready yet" for bigger responsibilities, even though you were his go-to for any crisis. You know the time when the promotion went to your white colleague instead, to the one who always came to work late. Oh, and of course you remember every time you did all the work and never got any credit. In my case, my career devastation happened when I had to walk away from my dream job because I didn't have any advocates willing to support their only Black woman colleague. When I needed them the most, my supposed friends wouldn't speak up. If we are honest with ourselves, we've often desperately tried to forget these workplace experiences because they hurt so badly. If we aren't careful, all of those years of so-and-so not meaning any harm will eventually catch up and cause us even more damage. We won't ever be able to be right within if we don't admit we've accumulated lots of workplace baggage during the toughest moments in our careers. Racialized trauma in the workplace is just as insidious as any other form of harassment. Yet Black and Brown pain seems to be something some white people don't want to acknowledge. Therefore, we have been conditioned to view our pain the same way they do: as nonexistent.

Additionally, culturally speaking, I believe there may be a common practice across communities of color where we are taught to silence our pain. We've learned to "hush up" when that crazy relative gets noticeably tipsy during the holidays, even when they make us uncomfortable. And we've learned not to "tell" when someone in our family might have harmed us.

Many people of color have gone through life being told the greatest hits: "Just be happy you have a good-paying job," "Make it work," and "Keep your head down." Unfortunately, we haven't always been encouraged to speak about the pain that we have experienced, especially pain related to the workplace. It's almost like we've let society convince us that racialized work trauma doesn't count. In the Black community especially, we are often told that racism at work is "just the way it is." If you are told a lie enough times, eventually you might just believe it. And many of us have believed that lie and passed it along to others. The ugly truth is, too many of us have the scars to prove it.

I wish I could help you let go of the baggage from every bad situation that has ever happened to you or someone you love; yet the gift I can give to you, the skill of packing light, might help you on your journey in the workplace today. The gift of potentially healing from workplace trauma, in my opinion, is better than any holiday or birthday present. *Right Within* is what I wish someone had given me when I was starting my climb up the workplace ladder. May this book serve as a resource that you can return to whenever you might need help along your journey to healing.

When I was four years old, I was in an unfortunate car accident that left a visible scar below my left eye. It's a scar I have grown to love, and it's part of who I am. The injuries I have from past toxic-workplace experiences, which I believe were racialized, led to scars that I learned to hide, and no amount of Neosporin can heal them. They are cuts that I wish I never had to endure. You might not know that these internalized scars are even there. But I would bet money that your invisible scars are the ones that hurt the most. The funny thing is, when we have external scars, there are bandages to aid the healing process. Why wouldn't we need resources for those racialized bruises too? News flash: learning to have tough skin doesn't heal you any faster; it just prolongs the pain.

I love the work of Dr. Thema Bryant-Davis, a tenured professor at Pepperdine University. She has conducted in-depth research around racial trauma. In her book *Healing Requires Recognition*, she says we must consider both the impact of the "systems and institutions that devalue members of one's race" and the impact of violations "being minimized or ignored because of one's race." It's not lost on me that the emotional scars we will discuss may be triggering for you, and I apologize. Even learning to address our pain may mean reopening old wounds caused by negative workplace experiences—a painful process in and of itself. Too many of us have been in workplaces that never bothered to extend to us the same level of professionalism and care that is extended toward our white colleagues. One thing that can help to overcome the gaslighting—the denial of our experience—that we've endured is recognizing among ourselves that our workplace traumas are real. These are violations that I wish companies, academic institutions, government agencies, and organizations would take seriously. The human resources department would never tell an employee who was physically assaulted at work that her attacker didn't mean any harm. Yet somehow it's acceptable to say to a woman of color who has been victimized because of her race, *It's just Bob being Bob and you are being too sensitive.* I am tired of this line of thinking, and I am officially implementing a no-tolerance memorandum for any institutions or corporations that do not take racialized aggression or trauma seriously.

We have to unlearn the idea that our racialized trauma doesn't matter. Those companies and organizations can't undo the past, but—whether we choose to speak up or not, whether these companies step up or not—it can still be empowering to take charge of what we can control. We can empower ourselves by centering our experiences and prioritizing our healing. In fact, the healing can start with us. But, with that said, we can and should hold companies and organizations accountable for creating a safe work environment where women of color can thrive and not just survive. Creating an equitable work environment that is free of racialized aggression is 100 percent their problem to solve. And their first step might be not letting Bob just continue to be Bob, because Bob's authentic self is harming others. And that should no longer be tolerated, no matter how nice of a guy Bob is to the higher-ups or how good his golf swing might be.

MY WHY

While I was on tour for my first book, *The Memo*, I met thousands of Black women and other women of color who appeared to still be grappling with many of their past and current workplace "broken hearts." In my first book, I posed a question in the chapter called "The Ugly Truth": "Where do the broken hearts of women of color go when we can't take it any longer?" That was the most quoted line from city to city, via email and social media. After the first ten cities, I realized there were recurring issues: unaddressed racial workplace trauma, the need for its recognition, and a lack of models of healing. Too often, healing had not yet taken place because we hadn't even allowed ourselves time to heal. Or perhaps we didn't even know we needed to heal, and therefore found it challenging to understand what it would look like. Many of us carry workplace baggage from job to job and position to position, which ultimately prevents us from adequately securing our seat at the table. And some of us are currently working in toxic environments that seem to prevent us from being able to heal, because we are triggered daily by the pain and the people that cause it.

I know from personal experience that, even if you change jobs, even if you move across the country, you can't keep avoiding your past. If you don't face this trauma head-on, it's just another bag you have to carry that was never supposed to be yours in the first place. I believe as women of color we have to heal from this workplace trauma because our health and wellness depend upon it. Not to mention, it becomes a heavy load to bear, and it's not our job to carry four-hundred-plus years of racial oppression. It's time we gather our tools to pack lighter and learn how to be right within, because our ancestors are begging us to. They had so many racialized bags that they were forced to carry that the stress alone killed many of them. We have the opportunity to turn our trauma into our most significant advantage: freedom. Audre Lorde said, "When I dare to be powerful, to use my strength in the service of my vision, then it becomes less and less important whether I am afraid." Healing can be scary, but we must be willing to push aside our caution and see how powerful we can be as women of color without all this extra sh*t weighing us down.

BEWARE OF FEELING LIKE YOU DON'T DESERVE IT

For many women of color, before we can ease on down the workplace road and get our seat at the table, we first need to heal. But how do you learn to be right within when you have settled into the microaggressions? Or perhaps you're accustomed to trying to make a toxic workplace work. It's not easy to heal, but we owe it to ourselves to try. As much as I want you to secure your seat at the table, I want you to make sure you are right within first. I want you to know what it feels like to be *free* at work. Webster's dictionary defines freedom as "the absence of necessity, coercion, or constraint in choice or action." Wouldn't it finally feel good to experience freedom at work? Freedom from the stereotypes of an Angry Black Woman, Feisty Latina, or Docile Asian? Don't you want to be released from the past triggers or the current toxicity that you may not even know is causing you pain? Here's another way to look at freedom. Billie Holiday had a song called "Good Morning Heartache." She sang, "I've got those Monday blues / Straight to Sunday blues." I don't want us to feel like we have to say good morning to the trauma, good afternoon to the trauma, or see you tomorrow, trauma! Trauma can't go where you're going. Your future can't sustain it. And you shouldn't be expected to normalize your racial trauma. All of that stops now, and I'm asking you to trust me when I tell you there's a lighter load on the other side. You deserve to know what healing feels like. And you deserve to know what tools you can use to pack a little bit lighter at work.

YOU ARE NOT ALONE

First things first: you are not alone, nor are you broken. We all have to allow ourselves time to heal so that we can maintain our "Empire State of Mind": that you can make it anywhere. I want you to be able to dismantle the mindset of systemic oppression that might have you questioning every room you enter, physical or virtual. In 2014, I realized that I was in desperate need of healing when I left my former employer and never gave myself the proper time to recover from many of my workplace broken hearts. I had dealt with an extremely racialized workplace situation, but I gave my notice, and within thirty days I had a new job. As Jay-Z said, "I'm on to the next one." I didn't give myself time to grieve a dream that I had to defer because of a toxic, racialized workplace. Racism doesn't just kill people; it kills careers too. Looking back, I almost needed a funeral to mourn the dream position that was forced into an early grave. I won't lie and say I am not still bothered by it, but I have learned not to be defined by that loss, because I found healing. Bad characters in the workplace had smothered my dream position because no one held them accountable—not even me. I was so tired of fighting that I made the best decision for my sanity and left it all behind. I never got the opportunity to mourn the pieces of me that were scattered across that office, and those are pieces of myself I will never get back. But the good news is, since then, I have grown and found new pieces of myself. And, today, I can honestly say that I feel like a brand new me—a version of myself that feels right within.

Many of us go through traumatic workplace experiences and then jump directly into a new role. Oh, and Black women, we have learned to make it do what it do! We don't have time to cry over spilled milk; we grab the paper towels, clean it up, and keep it moving. Yet, that isn't always the healthiest way to go about it. Unfortunately, it's become a survival mechanism for many of us—no judgment here. In those thirty days, I moved to another state and into a new apartment. I never had time to sulk; bills had to be paid. My responsibilities didn't stop because that job didn't work out. Maybe you have found yourself in a similar situation. Sometimes we feel like we have no other choice but to keep the ship moving. We have told ourselves that this is what's expected of us. But, what if I had given myself just a little time in between to breathe? Instead, I took my pain, threw it in my bag, and went to the next job. I took all sorts of things with me: guilt, shame, anxiety. I was paranoid as hell that there might be another situation like the one I left, so I shrank a bit. But, at the time, I didn't know how to articulate the pain or process it. And with that pain, I entered another workplace.

It wasn't as toxic as the last, but it sure was terrible. And this so-called strong Black woman ended up bursting into tears in my manager's office because I had suppressed fifteen years of racialized pain, and it finally caught up with me. I cried in his office, not just because of what he said and did that afternoon, but because of what every workplace had said, and because of what my past workplaces hadn't said when it was time to have my back. I have to admit, I never planned on crying a river that day, and Justin Timberlake was no-where to be found. It was just me, myself, and I. And when I walked out of my manager's office, I knew that I couldn't continue in my current state of pain. I had to deal with the workplace trauma once and for all. I don't want your trauma catching up with you the way mine did; I want you to learn how to slay your racialized trauma so that it no longer has control over you.

When I think back to that exact moment, it still hurts, but I am not paralyzed or embarrassed by it any longer. Right now you might even be thinking, *Minda, tell us more about that situation. It sounds kind of like the situation I'm in right now.* I promise, I will never leave you hanging, and if you continue reading, then you will find out exactly what went down that day in his corner office.

That day, I realized that there are workplace situations that I thought I was over, yet the wounds were still fresh. Yes, I was functional, but I suffered from the side effects of racial workplace trauma. It's hard to bring your authentic self to work when you haven't learned to be right within. Because, let's face it, when we experience so much trauma, we no longer know what it means to be ourselves. All the hurt has transformed us into another person. And when we hang onto those toxic bags and bring them home after work, some of our family and friends end up on the receiving end of our trauma. So you see, our trauma doesn't affect just us but everyone who loves us too. Maybe you don't want to pack lighter for yourself, but would you consider being right within for your child, partner, or best friend? Either way, it goes, healing is a state I'd love to have you visit, and if you don't like how healing feels, please feel free to pick up all your racialized suitcases from baggage claim at the carousel labeled Workplace Hell.

I SAID WHAT I SAID

Maybe you aren't ready to heal—I get it! Healing can be ugly. It can be messy, but I promise you, healing will always be worth it. And if you have never given yourself permission to center yourself and your feelings, then healing might not seem like a priority to you. Perhaps none of what I have said thus far is your story. Or maybe it's not that you need to heal from past workplace trauma. Maybe you're thinking, *Chile, I need to heal from current workplace trauma.* I got you covered with tools to help heal those pains too. Or maybe you are one of those people who feel like you have it all under control and you've moved on from those experiences and it is what it is. No matter the situation, and I hate to assume, but I bet you've had your share of disappointments in the workplace related to race that you've tried to forget. Or you might have told yourself the same narrative that some white people hope we cling to: that our trauma isn't racially charged. I got something in this book for you too, because there was a time I thought I had everything under control and I already told you where that thinking got me—nowhere.

We can no longer support systemic ideologies that don't center dignity and humanity for women of color in the workplace. If race didn't play a role in our advancement, there would be more women of color meaningfully featured in companies and organizations, and not just in their stock photography. I secured my seat at the table, but I had so much racialized baggage that it caused PTSD (post-traumatic stress disorder) and I felt triggered daily. And that is no way to live our best career life. So, again, we all might be experiencing the workplace differently, but I guarantee that there are some common issues we have shared and that healing might make a difference for our future of work.

As I mentioned before, the road to healing isn't for the faint of heart. Just like any transformation, the journey takes work. There might be times throughout this book when you just have to drop down to your knees and ask the good Lord for some strength to keep moving toward your happy place, because those experiences have become too painful to recount. Yet, I want you to know I am here with you so that you don't have to go through this journey alone. I, too, had to make a pilgrimage to find a place of workplace healing. One of my favorite poems is one that Louisiana native Jessica D. Gallion created for a private event at my company, The Memo LLC. In "Holding a Seat at the Table of Gratitude," Jessica writes, "Tell your demon to get off your back, ask the ancestors to get louder, when you're backed into a corner, because it's all on you." Later in her poem, she says, "Tell them you were born for this, and there ain't no rules, and it's all-new, shout it over and over again." Listen, if those words didn't make you want to hop up off your couch and shout me down, we might need to check your pulse. You better tell those workplace demons to get out your bag. Healing might be new, but guess what, my friend, it's all on you. And I know, you know, you deserve it. And I bet healing would look really great on you if you just allowed yourself to test it out.

NOW WHAT

I will share stories of the workplace trauma that almost caused me to give up on my dreams entirely, and I will share how I learned to pack lighter. A key lesson from my journey is that success is not a solo sport. I couldn't play the role of both healer and patient. And knowing what I know now, that isn't even possible! I needed a squad of people invested in my mental workplace success. Trying to solve your problems alone is a short-term coping mechanism. I am going to pull back the curtain and show you what healing looked like for me. I realize our roads might not look the same, but I will share some of the tools that helped me make it to the other side of sanity. I used many tools and frameworks to become right within and be the best version of myself. I had to choose myself, which is one of the greatest acts of self-love. I knew my health depended on continuous healing practices, and I will share those practices as well.

There are some topics I think we should discuss before we jump to the how-to part of this book, such as understanding the history of healing. What does healing even mean in a cultural context? We will also explore what faith leaders say about healing and how the church can play an active role in the mental health of Black women and other women of color. In particular, we will see how the Black church has been an enormous source of strength for Black women since slavery. And we will also discuss how the church might have failed many of us when it comes to our mental health. It's something I've wanted to explore because I grew up in the church. What many of you probably don't know about me is that I am a PK, a pastor's kid. So I have a lot of thoughts about the Black church. But I won't just explore my faith, which is Christianity. We will also explore some approaches to healing from other religions, because not all women of color identify as Christian, though a large majority of us do.

Additionally, I will share insights on healing through therapy. It's another tool in our healing tool kit, and here I'll bring you sage and scientific advice from some of the country's leading Black women therapists. Unfortunately, therapy hasn't always been celebrated by communities of color. And since there is so much stigma around going to see a therapist, I had to make therapy its own chapter. I remember when I decided to go to see a therapist for the first time. I told one of my relatives, and they shamed me for even considering it because they didn't think I was "crazy." Okay, let's just jump into the deep end of the pool, shall we? Language like that is very damning. From that day forward, I never mentioned it again, but I did seek therapy. As a matter of fact, I didn't talk about it for years, especially with other Black people. I felt this sense of judgment. Yet with my white friends, we would kiki all about our therapy sessions—therapy is a tool many of them are encouraged to take advantage of.

And with that said, there's another truth: in the Black community, we often don't have the same access to mental health care and wellness as our counterparts. We are conditioned to think only "crazy" people go to therapy, not fully understanding the range of situations that it can help. Someone who has been diagnosed as bipolar might use therapy, and the person who just needs someone to listen might use it too. I view both parties as winning because they understand we can't always help ourselves by ourselves. Neither should be ashamed for using a tool that allows them to be right within. I went to therapy for three years and stopped. Then I started back up again after a work experience went horribly awry. I see therapy as an additional way to enhance one's psychological safety. And I hope you will be open to some of the tools we will discuss throughout the book and pick up the ones that you think might work for you.

The bottom line is, whatever route or combination you choose, I will support you every step of the way. There isn't a one-size-fits-all approach to healing from racialized workplace trauma. For some of us, healing might happen in a jumping-jack flash, for others, it might take years, and for others, it might be small acts of courage our entire lives—but no matter what, our emotional well-being will be better for it.

EVERY LITTLE STEP YOU TAKE

I don't want you to look at this book as just another self-help or career book. Naw, don't play me like that. I care too much about your mental health to give you just any advice. And we are both mature enough to admit that healing isn't prescriptive. I can't tell you to spin around ten times and holler out the names of the people who wronged you, and bam, you're healed! Although now that I think about it, it could be something you might want to try. All jokes aside, healing takes courage. And small acts of courage go a long way. With the resources you find in *Right Within*, please know that you are in the driver's seat, and you can view me as your driver's ed instructor. I will be sitting in the passenger seat, ready to hit the emergency brake if you need me to. Ultimately, you get to decide what works best for you. I just ask that you permit yourself to explore the possibilities. And take your time. You don't have to rush through this book. My hope is that you take time to marinate and meditate after each chapter. Don't be afraid to ask yourself the tough questions in order to reach your breakthrough.

And once you begin to make progress, we will discuss maintenance. Because as much as I hope you will never encounter another toxic workplace, the reality is, not every manager or colleague has the tools to be their best self. We might be on the receiving end of their trauma. And in that case, you might have to break them off with a copy of this book and get your office book club popping.

INCLUSIVITY

Additionally, as you can already tell from reading or listening to this book, I tend to use both "women of color" and "Black women" when describing a workplace situation. I use "women of color" when I want to be more inclusive of the experiences of a broader group of women. Meaning, women who identify as Black, Brown, Indigenous, or a person of color. And I use "Black women" when I am describing an experience that might be more specific to Black culture. I identify as a Black woman and many of the experiences that I write about tend to be ones that other Black women have had as well. I have also decided to use the traditional spelling of the word "woman" or "women," yet this book is meant for any person who identifies as a woman. I don't discriminate and all women are welcome at my table—including white women. I care about using language in an inclusive way, and the language around diversity is constantly shifting, so I wanted to be clear about my use of language in this book so the message is not lost.

Oh, and before I forget: I am not the only one who has made it through toxic workplace terrors. I will share stories of other women of color who went through hell to get to their heaven. I told you, you are not alone. I think we have waited long enough to address the pain; it's time to rewrite your narrative and redefine who you want to be going forward, with some healing methods in your tool kit. Lastly, I've included some reflection areas after each chapter to help you think through some of the emotions that might come up. Feel free to use the prompts throughout the book to guide you on your new journey. But let me tell you: you've now reached the no-BS zone. Healing works when we're honest with ourselves. Bishop T. D. Jakes said it best, "God wants you to be healed so you can go on."

I firmly believe that in order for us to experience a workplace that works for us, we have to be right within so we aren't bogged down by the trauma. And healing doesn't have to be something that only repairs a limb or cures a disease; healing can be whatever you need it to be. You get to define that for yourself. I can't tell you what healing should be like; I can only present you with some stories, insights, advice, options, and tools. And if at any time, you feel like the work is too hard, that is when I want you to reach out and connect with a larger community, including the one I have created. We can help each other heal as a community. In the back of this book, I have resources that will help you continue to heal with purpose.

Because success is not a solo sport, let's make sure we get this book into the hands of anyone who has ever experienced racialized workplace trauma. We can't be the only ones receiving our healing—friends don't let friends weigh themselves down with bags of trauma. In the words of my friend in my head, Beyoncé, "Won't let my freedom rot in hell / Hey! Imma keep running / 'cause a winner don't quit on themselves." And you are a winner, and I know you won't quit on this healing journey. Because too much is at risk if you don't even try. But first, the one question I want to ask you: What could healing from racialized workplace trauma look like for you? Once you've had a chance to think about that, I will be waiting for you over in Chapter 2.

Chapter 2

ADDRESSING THE PAIN

I smile, even though I hurt see I smile
I know God is working so I smile
—Kirk Franklin, "I Smile"

For me, healing is still taking place. There were times in my career when I thought I had finished healing, and then I'd find myself triggered by a new racialized experience and it would set me right back where I started—traumatized. To be fair, had I understood what healing truly meant, I would have incorporated some maintenance strategies, because healing requires maintenance. And healing takes *a lot* of self-work.

There were two significant moments in my career that brought me to my knees. They were racialized experiences that I wouldn't wish on my enemies. But before I tell you about those two incidents, I have to ask you a few questions. I feel the need to ask you about them now, because I will check in with you throughout our journey together and see if your answers have evolved.

1. What does healing mean to you?
2. Do you believe you've ever experienced workplace trauma due to racism?
3. Are you open to exploring various tools to help you achieve healing?

Thank you for answering these questions. For some of you, they might have brought up some past workplace broken hearts. Yet I want to reiterate that this book is a safe space, and you can be vulnerable. You can let your hair down or keep it up. There are no rules on how you choose to heal. And as I mentioned in the previous chapter, my only ask is that you keep an open mind to what healing could look like for you.

SYSTEMS OF OPPRESSION

Let me put it to you this way. For so long, these systems of oppression have been embedded in most workplace cultures. These systems were never created to support me or you. And these systems have been strategically created to have us believe that we are crazy and that we have either made up racism or don't have thick enough skin. And when the dominant narrative has been crammed down our throats for hundreds of years as a community, we start to believe that we might be crazy and that we might be the problem. And let us not forget, this same system is an often invisible one that is coded and steeped in white supremacy. And that, folks, is how systemic racism was meant to operate— to make us question ourselves. We must never forget that.

That is why it's so important we dismantle systems that don't serve us.

With those facts alone, you deserve a little healing. We deserve to heal because many of our ancestors never got the chance to heal from their racialized trauma. They died with trauma in their bones and on their lips. I had to write this book so we don't add you to those statistics. Let's start a new data set, one that includes our healing rate. Because let's be honest, the alternative is going through life wounded. Do you want that for yourself? Of course not!

Others might fall into the camp of, *As long as I am making money, who cares about what I have to endure?* Trust me—that isn't the move either. Money doesn't provide healing for the long term. It's only a cheap Band-Aid from the ninety-nine-cent store. And you know those don't work for long. I know firsthand what it's like to make a six-figure salary and be miserable at work. And not because I didn't like my job—oh, I loved my job. I just didn't like how my manager treated me. As I reflect on too many racialized occurrences to count, I am not sure how I survived traditional workplaces for fifteen years. My previous job should provide me with health insurance to unpack all the unnecessary trauma I experienced on their watch, because some of my trauma still needs to be removed on their dime.

UNDER THE RUG

I want so badly for you to understand how vital healing is for your overall career health. I probably sound like a broken record, and we are only in the second chapter, but I don't mind being that for you. Your mental and career health is important to me. I want you to use some of my work experiences as a cautionary tale.

I was starting to become one of those Black women who swept my racialized experiences under the rug at the expense of my own well-being. Alex, I will take Workplace Oppression for $500. What is, Isn't that what all women of color are supposed to do? And Alex (may his soul rest in peace) politely looks at me and says, "Oh, no, sorry." But all jokes aside, here are some of the things I swept under the rug that darn sure should have been on top of that rug for everyone to see:

1. My manager saw that I was wearing burnt-orange nail polish, and he decided it was appropriate to joke for fifteen minutes about how Black people love bright colors.

2. I started a new client project, and when I arrived, my new manager said, "Now I have someone to make my coffee for me in the morning. I like it black."

3. Another manager called me incompetent, yet he always asked me to execute high-profile client meetings or projects.

4. One of my managers asked me to "take one for the team" when one of my colleagues dropped the ball and blamed me to save themselves in front of a client I worked closely with. It fractured the relationship I had with the client.

Those are just some of my racialized workplace experiences, and number four probably hurt the most—it is one of the career experiences that brought me to my knees. It was also the straw that broke the camel's back, which caused me to give my notice, and I haven't looked back since.

HEALING TAKES TIME

I hate to have to tell you this, but healing from racial trauma might not happen overnight. Well, at least it took a lot longer for me. So I hope you will try to look at it as a marathon, because your healing is always going to be a slow, progressive change. Any change that comes about too quickly, most likely, will result in a false sense of security. Please take the time to heal and run your race. Healing is not an after-school special over in an hour—it's just the beginning. And I have to admit something else to you: after just two years in corporate America, I experienced so much racism at work that I began to think it was normal—hence how I was able to sweep it under the rug. I no longer batted an eye when someone white said something out of pocket or inappropriate to me or about me. It got so bad on most days that if I made it a few hours without some racialized comment, I considered it a good day, just like Ice Cube—that is, before his failed Contract with Black America. No woman should have to go through their workday with wins like that.

I was often the only Black woman in the room, and I figured if I was going to survive, I'd better learn how to smile through the absurdity. You know those times when Chad or

Cindy says something racially charged, intentionally or unintentionally. Then one of two scenarios takes place: (1) everyone laughs, or (2) there's an awkward silence and we move on to the next agenda item as if there was nothing to see here.

As women of color, we learn to smile differently in the workplace. We learn how to smile to keep from crying because no one in that room felt it necessary to humanize us and our experiences. White colleagues can see and empathize with the pain of women who look like their daughters or sisters, but they can't seem to recognize our pain. They swear they don't want to see the "angry" Black woman come out and play, yet they're always testing us to see if she might show up. This is not a remake of *Candyman*. This is about our lived experience, and their ignorance impacts our careers. Not only are we racially insulted, but now colleagues who we thought were friends pretend nothing offensive took place. Or if they do mention it, they say no harm was intended. How do we know what Chad intended if no one ever brings it to his attention? I'm glad everyone can speak for Chad and Cindy, but why can't anyone ever speak up for me? In the words of public academic and lecturer Rachel Cargle, "I don't want your love and light if it doesn't come with solidarity and action. I have no interest in passive empathy."

This brings us to another question we must wrestle with: Why do some white people give more care and humanity to those who are causing the offense than to those who are on the receiving end of the offense? Real harm is being caused inside of the workplace due to racial aggression, and in order to have an equitable workplace, these offenses must be taken seriously. Most people don't leave a workplace because they no longer like their job; they leave because of a colleague or manager. And what bothers me the most is that while women of color often have to leave a toxic workplace, the wrongdoers often get to stay and continue on, ready to harm the next person. Where does the buck stop?

BUT THEY MEAN WELL

What drives me up and down the wall is when our white colleagues feel the need to tell us such trash, when they should be telling Cindy to stop oppressing folks like me. And if we are being candid, if the Cindys and Chads of the workplace are saying racist things, you best believe they're probably saying some sexist or homophobic stuff too. Pretending that the harm doesn't exist doesn't make women of color feel better; it isolates us further. Eventually, this diminishment of our feelings becomes one more weight we have to carry at work. In the interview process, I don't believe anyone mentioned I'd have to deal with such insensitive colleagues. And I don't recall the job posting saying anything about having to walk on eggshells each day so no one thinks I am angry or aggressive. Nor do I remember being told that I would spend so much of my energy coddling my white colleagues and managing the racialized crap coming out of their mouths during staff meetings and emails. Perhaps there should be a bonus given each year as a form of reparations. Because at what point is the workplace going to hit the emergency brake and give a damn about you, me, your momma, and your cousins too? We are always on the receiving end of these racialized comments and all of that harm eventually catches up to us. It ain't right, and there is no excuse for this type of behavior at work.

Meanwhile, after each incident, everyone else goes back to their work space and gets on social media to post another cat picture. We are left sitting at our desk, playing that horrible exchange on a loop in our head for the entire day. Some of us will take it a step further and beat ourselves up for not saying something in the moment. While navigating a toxic workplace, we are still expected to give everything we've got. Unfortunately, many of us ain't got much left. We are tired. And we aren't even able to do our job at full capacity due to racism. I wish our counterparts could walk a mile in our shoes for just two hours. I guarantee they would quickly become better allies.

For some of us, we can leave a toxic workplace and move to a new job to find space to heal. But for the rest of us, we must figure out what healing looks like from where we currently sit. The normalization of racialized trauma teaches many of us to just make it work—and when you can make it work, sometimes you overlook the pain. Once I took a step back and realized I was in pain, I wasn't sure if I could do the work that might be required of me in order to heal. I know, I know—we always have to be the ones doing the work, but this is work that will benefit us. It's the best work I have ever done, and I hope you will find healing beneficial to your career.

Quick question: What are some of the things you've swept under the rug? Whatever those things were, let's agree we can't afford to hide them anymore, because racism costs women of color too much, and it's time to be right within.

DOING THE WORK

I was having a conversation with Dr. Joy Harden Bradford, licensed psychologist and the host of the popular mental-health podcast *Therapy for Black Girls*. I asked Dr. Joy what healing meant to her. She responded this way: "Acknowledging things that have happened and figuring out how to make it part of your story without becoming your entire story." She went on to say that as Black women, it's essential to "understand how the trauma is impacting us so we can take care of it." Just so we are clear, deciding to do nothing probably isn't the best way of taking care of it. So let's build on addressing the pain. But before we can talk about the tools, we need to address what situations might have caused you pain or trauma in a way that left you feeling like you weren't the same person anymore.

I will start by giving you an example of how I began to address my pain. Let's take the burnt-orange nail polish situation and break it down.

1. **Who?** My former manager. Let's call him Chad Smith.
2. **What?** He singled me out for wearing burnt-orange nail polish and made a series of racialized comments in front of me and another colleague about how Black people love bright colors.
3. **Where?** I was driving him and my colleague around in a rental car while on a work errand.
4. **Why?** It wasn't the first time he had made racialized comments in my presence, and at the time I kept telling myself that he wasn't racist and he just didn't know any better. But the reality was he was a fully grown

adult who didn't live under a rock, and he should have known better. I remember never wanting to call him racist, but if the shoe fits, I guess Chad should wear it. I may never fully understand why he treated me this way. But I do believe he was trying to minimize and belittle me by gaining some weird attention for himself. Chad also knew that I wouldn't challenge him, because I didn't want to rock the boat.

I would encourage you to start with one of your painful racialized workplace experiences. Then, if you choose to investigate additional trauma caused in the workplace, please remember to be kind to yourself and take your time. Ask yourself the questions: Who? What? Where? Why? Consider this necessary information gathering. This exercise is one way to start acknowledging your pain, gathering information about your pain, and documenting your pain. Sometimes we don't permit ourselves to call a thing a thing—or, like Dr. Joy referenced, we don't allow ourselves to acknowledge our pain. Part of acknowledging our racialized pain is allowing ourselves to dig deeper.

When Chad made that comment to me, what was he really saying? It wasn't about the nail polish. He was signaling that he felt I was different, that Black people are different. Let's be honest, Black people aren't the only people in the world who like bright colors, and not every Black person likes bright colors. But again, it wasn't the colors—do you get what I am saying? If Chad could have such a biased opinion of Black people in this one example, what other stereotypes did he believe were real? As we are gathering our information, it's important to acknowledge what these microaggressions add up to: Would I ever have been able to rise up the ladder when working with colleagues like Chad? Probably not! In order to disrupt these systems, we must never normalize the behavior of Chads. We should normalize a narrative where people like Chad don't belong in workplaces that are striving to be equitable. With that said, you always belong. It's just the abusive people who don't.

I posed another key question to Dr. Joy: Why was it that some women of color haven't permitted themselves to heal. She reminded me that, historically, Black women in particular had not been encouraged to do so. Often our pain has been weaponized. We have been conditioned to be strong, from our ancestors' days on the plantations to the civil rights movement. All we knew was pain and trauma in the workplace.

It hasn't always been safe for us to air our grievances and embrace our pain. Meanwhile, white women have long been encouraged to be vulnerable. An example of this might be what some refer to as "white woman tears." White women may racially attack us, but if we speak up, too often they will claim that they are the true victims. The minute a white woman releases her tears, she starts to center herself and the game is over. Our concerns and trauma are immediately dismissed. Next thing you know, we have entered the oppression Olympics, and when white women come to the race, it's hard to win.

WHITE WOMAN TEARS

Since we are discussing white woman tears, this is a good time to tell you about one of the most painful times in my

career. It's the moment I realized that racism could potentially cost women of color our mental health if we allow it
to. Because racism almost cost me mine. I moved across the
country from the West Coast to the East Coast for what I
had thought was my dream job. In a matter of months, that
dream turned into a nightmare. I had a colleague named
Kerry who I had to work closely with. She was much older
than I was, and I imagined she probably knew where many
of the skeletons were hidden and might have hidden a few
herself. When Kerry first started to mistreat me, I did what
most of us do best: sweep it under the rug. Because you know
we don't want to believe someone is racist. I thought all those
people had died and gone to hell. Growing up, I always heard
how "those" people were going to die out and we would be
just fine. But these racialized demons aren't going anywhere.
They are running around like monsters in the "Thriller" video,
and many of us work with or for them.

Kerry started with micro-insults, took a quick left at microaggressions, and then drove head-on into blatant acts of
racism. I remember one time she invited me to attend an
event in a sales territory that we both shared. Kerry told me
that she would love to introduce me to some people and that
it would be a good opportunity for me. When she extended
this olive branch, I wanted to give her the benefit of the doubt.
I thought, *Okay maybe she isn't racist after all. Maybe I got it
wrong.* When I arrived, she said hello and then barely spoke
to me the rest of the evening, not introducing me to anyone.
There was a time when she made some short remarks, during
which she thanked everyone for coming and acknowledged
the colleagues, by name, who had come out and supported

her. She acknowledged all of her colleagues except me. Mind you, they all worked in a different department.

When I returned to the office, the narrative she painted was that she had introduced me to everyone and shown me the ropes. It couldn't have been further from the truth. Eventually, Kerry's attempts to isolate me with her callous behavior became more and more overt, and she became such a thorn in my side that I couldn't focus on my work. Everyone in our department watched as my mental health declined, but rather than speak up, they seemed to be waiting for me to leave. Kerry continued to push and push and push until I finally gave my notice and had to leave.

The position I had worked so hard for—the title and the money—may it rest in peace, because it died due to racism. I suffered mentally and psychologically. And when I did air my grievances, Kerry released her version of white woman tears and made the situation all about her and how she had tried her hardest to support me. She was like Donald Trump when he says that nobody has worked harder for African American people than he has. Yeah, her actions helped me—they helped me decide to pack my bags and leave. The ugly truth about racialized experiences in the workplace is that women of color end up deciding to leave due to the lack of psychological safety. Even when I reported the abuse to our manager, I was told to "suck it up." Kerry was never held accountable.

Racism in the workplace is like unregulated prescription drugs, and there are side effects. They read something like this: Working in a racially aggressive environment may cause headaches, panic attacks, self-doubt, and anxiety. In extreme cases, you might lose your job or leave your job. Please consult with an attorney. I left that place with so much racialized baggage I needed a U-Haul. At the time, I couldn't wrap my mind around the journey I'd need to take to finally heal from all of that.

WORKPLACE SAFETY

The idea of psychological safety at work was created by Amy Edmondson, Novartis professor of leadership and management at Harvard Business School. She defines a psychologically safe workplace as "one where people are not full of fear, and not trying to cover their tracks to avoid being embarrassed or punished." Once I started following Edmondson's work, I started to think long and hard about how healing is directly connected to a psychologically safe workplace. We would never debate that it's probably a bad idea to have someone who has a history of physically attacking colleagues continue on in the workplace. Physical safety should be an obvious company value. So why don't organizations take into consideration removing someone with a history of racially aggressing others in the workplace? Edmondson states, "Without psychological safety, there's greater risk of cutting corners and people getting hurt, whether employees, customers, or patients."

In my experience with Kerry, psychological safety was missing. Every level of our department's leadership failed me because they were friends with Kerry inside and outside of work. My grievances weren't taken seriously because my white colleagues said that they had never experienced her abuse, and they couldn't believe she would ever do that. Um, ma'am, sir, have you ever been a Black woman at work and had to deal with racially aggressive colleagues? If not, then you need to have several seats. Please spare me the BS. The thing is, two things can be correct at the same time. Kerry could be abusive to a Black colleague and still be a great friend to all her white colleagues. Somehow folks think that kindness toward some means kindness toward all.

In the end, we must hold leaders accountable for creating a workplace free of discrimination, in which *all* employees can do their work without fear of being attacked—period. When my colleagues refused to address the abuse I was experiencing, the only way I could find the safety I needed was by leaving my dream job. No human being should have to go through that type of psychological and racial abuse. From here, I need to share with you some ways companies can create a safe workplace. It is possible. I want you to know what "good" is supposed to look like, even if you haven't experienced it. The exposure to good workplace guidelines will help us on our road to being right within.

RESTORATIVE JUSTICE

Too many workplaces are exacerbating the racial drama instead of providing solutions for restoration. More companies and organizations have to acknowledge the role they have played in racialized trauma as it pertains to women of color in the workplace. At the bare minimum, they need to incorporate some restorative practices to dismantle their racialized workplace culture. I recommend *restoration agreements*. It's a term I have coined to set the tone in work environments.

Restoration agreements are meant to rebuild trust inside the workplace as it relates to unchecked racial aggression. Additionally, these agreements will help center those who have been racially harmed. Leaders and managers must incorporate some workplace norms that benefit everyone, not just the dominant majority. Here are some ways to incorporate workplace restoration agreements to help restore racialized safety.

Team Meetings

I find that many racialized occurrences happen in staff or team meetings. Personally, large team meetings are where I have experienced the most microaggressions. For example, never being able to get a word in. Or the infamous dismissing your idea and then passing it off as their own. Oh and of course, those inappropriate jokes or slurs that casually roll off your colleagues' tongues. This is an opportunity for you to take a leadership role if you choose. You can start by suggesting rules of engagement to your manager when it comes to their team's meeting culture. Only you know what type of norms are needed to offset the nonsense.

Your manager could start by assigning a meeting advisor who monitors the tone of the meetings and manages the toxic behavior that might take place. The meeting advisor would observe the team's actions, language, and tone, then pass their notes along to their manager. This is an opportunity to make managers aware of some disturbing behaviors. Often, managers are already aware of some of the issues, but they haven't bothered to have a formalized space to address them. The practice of documenting issues holds managers accountable as well. And it doesn't have to all be bad news. The advisor can also commend those who encourage others to speak and who amplify what others say to make sure they are credited for their ideas. This way, people in the meeting are acutely aware of their behavior and, as my elders would say, they will "mind their business." Sometimes we have to create an understanding of what behavior is encouraged and what behavior won't be tolerated. As you begin to incorporate restoration agreements into your work culture, you will find additional ways to make meetings a psychologically safe space.

Promotions

Another area where I see an opportunity to use restoration agreements is in the hiring process. Part of psychological safety in the workplace boils down to who companies are hiring and promoting. For example, currently Black women account for 1.4 percent of the executive suite in corporate America. Clearly there are more talented Black women in the workforce, yet we are not being retained and advanced. I have been a Black woman my entire life, and I know the heartache related to always being passed up for the promotion that you just knew was yours, only to hear, "It wasn't your time" or "Be patient." While I was being patient, white person after white person was elevated, and I continued to work my butt off with little hope of advancement.

This is a psychologically unsafe environment for people of color. That is not just my feeling, but the facts. Look at the diversity reports companies put out every year—dismal movement when it comes to Black and Brown women. Today, leadership could make a restoration agreement that they will no longer move forward with a hire until the interview pool is diverse and the people on the hiring committee are also diverse. If you don't have any people in your organization who are diverse and can be part of the hiring team, then you definitely have two problems that need to be addressed. Restoration agreements aren't just good to have; they are imperative for equality.

Organizational Culture

According to the Society for Human Resource Management, organizational culture is "the proper way to behave within the organization. This culture consists of shared beliefs and values established by leaders and then communicated and reinforced through various methods, ultimately shaping employee perceptions, behaviors and understanding." And if the organizational culture perpetuates an unsafe environment for employees, then what does that say about the leadership? Nevertheless, *all* colleagues contribute to the organizational culture; it's not just on the CEO. A work culture that is silent when abuse is present is a culture that passively perpetuates abuse. You can see this dramatized on the Apple TV series *The Morning Show*, starring Steve Carell, Reese Witherspoon, and Jennifer Aniston. One of the anchors, Mitch (Steve Carell), gets fired for sexually harassing a female assistant. In one scene, Mitch storms into the conference room and blasts his former colleagues because they had known what he was doing and never said anything. He said that when he was still employed at the station, everyone knew, yet they even went out for drinks with him. For years, they were showing him that his behavior was allowed by never calling him on it. All of us have seen this kind of permissiveness harm women, people of color, or queer colleagues.

One way I believe restoration agreements could help organizational culture is by providing managers with the proper training. Most managers are not equipped to manage diverse talent, so they tend to shy away from anything they perceive as race related. The workforce is changing, and we can't afford managers any more time to grow into their emotional intelligence. Too many women of color suffer while their managers are trying to improve. Managers need tools on how to create a safe environment for their staff. Which brings us to an important point: training for conflict resolution. Managers should be trained on how to identify, navigate, and have conversations around microaggressions when they are happening in the workplace. I would guess that an overwhelming majority of women of color experience racial aggression on some level every day at work, so why wouldn't there be company-wide management training? And bystander training for employees of all levels? It is going to be hard as hell for us to heal if our employers don't put up the necessary guardrails to help us maintain our healing and mental health.

PRIORITIZING SAFETY

If you haven't figured it out by now, I believe in being a little radical when necessary. I think that part of managers' annual evaluations should include how they have handled racialized workplace occurrences. If they are not providing safety for everyone on the team, then there should be some repercussions. Executives have to prioritize psychological safety for everyone on their staff. And it shouldn't be on women of color to dismantle a workplace's racism; we have to be given much-needed space to heal from past abuses. If a workplace is predominately white, then the dominant group needs to take on the task of doing the anti-racist work of addressing our pain.

The workplace should be a safe place for women of color, but it has failed many of us. I appreciate the work of Amy Edmondson because it can be expanded upon in a racialized context. She makes a point that "without psychological safety, diversity does not automatically mean people can bring their full selves to work." If women of color can't bring their government names, hairstyles, or identities into the workplace without fear of backlash or isolation, then workplaces need to be shut down like the health department shuts down a restaurant when it is not up to code. Sometimes it starts with a fine, or it might receive one of those horrible grades like a C or D. I don't know about you, but I never eat at a B, C, or D restaurant, and I sure as hell don't want to work at a place with such low standards for equity.

INTERVENTION

Addressing our pain is a form of liberation. Audre Lorde said, "I write for those women who do not speak, for those who do not have a voice because they were so terrified because we are taught to respect fear more than ourselves." One way to address our pain is through using our voices and through courageous conversations. When I was going through my struggle with Kerry, I had colleagues I thought were friends, but none of them ever stood up for me. They mostly would come behind closed doors and tell me how they felt sorry for me and how strong they thought I was being. But what I really needed was for them to speak up in meetings or maybe even go to the human resources department when they observed bad behavior. During that time in my life, I always thought Kerry was the problem. I was only able to direct my frustration toward her. Yet all of my colleagues who saw something and said nothing were just as much at fault. On my journey to healing, I also had to address that part of my pain as well. Those bystanders saw the racialized abuse and chose to do nothing about it.

I was talking to attorney Kelly Charles-Collins about bystander intervention in the workplace. Charles-Collins helps keep companies and organizations on the right side of those hashtag movements and provides specialized training around bystander intervention in the workplace. She says bystanders in the workplace can de-escalate or disrupt discrimination and bullying when they see it taking place. She explained, "Colleagues need to activate their allyship by remembering that we are all human." She went on to say that our white colleagues don't have to completely save the day, but there are always actions they can do to protect us. It amazes me how some of our colleagues think that their ignorance will protect them. Meaning, if they pretend they don't know what is going on or if they don't think someone is being racist, then they can somehow wash their hands of it all. The Kerry enablers are just as much at fault.

I asked Charles-Collins what our colleagues could do to intervene when they see something racialized happening. Here are two tips she gave to those who want to help provide a psychologically safe environment when they see their colleagues racially assaulted:

- **Make Good Trouble.** Colleagues have to shift away from this mindset of *I don't want to cause trouble.* The trouble has already been caused. You are being selfish by only thinking about yourself. Charles-Collins suggests asking yourself this question: "What would you do if this was happening to someone you love or if it was happening to you? What would you want someone to do for you? Then do the same thing." It boils down to being a decent human being at work. We are sure you wouldn't want someone to just sit there and do nothing. And think about what you're going to do when you see it happening next time, because there will be a next time.

- **You Don't Have to Be the Hero.** Charles-Collins also mentioned that as a bystander you don't have to be the hero, but you have to do something. You have to consider the full spectrum of possible responses and figure out the best strategy to move everyone forward. We all have a responsibility to intervene when we see something happen. Some may choose to use their voice, some might protest, and others might hire Charles-Collins to come in and help them figure out how to incorporate effective bystander intervention.

One of my biggest regrets in my former workplace was giving my colleagues a pass for not doing anything to provide a safe place for me to work. I often think about how I might still be thriving in my dream job if one person would have intervened on my behalf. I had an office full of adults who were too busy with their lives to talk to me, at least until it was time for them to ask me to buy Girl Scout cookies or candles for their child's school fundraiser. Oh how I wish I had been more courageous and told my colleagues that it's not enough to come to me privately and feel sorry for me when I was being abused. I wish I had told them the ways I needed them to show up for me. I didn't think I had the agency to say that. And, let's be honest, I shouldn't have had to say it. As I continue to heal, I might decide to write them all a letter that I never mail, just to release myself from the pain they caused. But in the meantime, maybe you can identify someone you consider an advocate on your team who can help you navigate those uncomfortable moments at work. When you start to go down the healing road, you begin to unpack all the areas that need to be addressed. Like DJ D-Nice says, "Sometimes you gotta let it breathe."

EQUITY ADVOCATES

Okay, here I go again with my radical thinking, but please hear me out: What if there were people on our teams that we pre-identify as *equity advocates*? These advocates would commit to showing up for anyone on the margins in the workplace: in meetings, at lunch, or anywhere on work time when someone is being othered or they notice the workplace is not safe for their colleagues. Do you know how revolutionary that could be? Do you think Chad or Cindy is going to cut up in a meeting when they know someone will hold them accountable? Hell no. I guarantee they will act right, quick and fast.

I know what you might be thinking: What would this even look like, Minda? I am so glad you asked. Let's say that your manager has identified some people on your team who have communicated that they would like more managerial experience or stretch opportunities. Your manager could ask them if they would like to serve as an equity advocate and be a leader on the team. This would require them to show up for their colleagues in the ways I mentioned earlier. By giving them these opportunities, it helps them be part of the solution and de-escalates racialized behavior on the team. This could also be something that is housed in the human resources department, which could train and recruit these advocates. There are so many opportunities to get everyone on board.

Essentially, my hope is that eventually there would be no need for this because the expectation would be set that equity and respect is an important pillar of a company's workplace culture. There would be a clear understanding that if any employee fails to agree with that, then perhaps this isn't the right workplace for them. And with that, I just went to workplace heaven. But this aspiration needs to become our reality. The task for managers is not easy. Dismantling these systems will take revolutionary acts. Equity advocates can support not only women of color but also other marginalized employees; their work could result in a more equitable environment for everyone. We should all strive to be equity advocates and make the workplace better for our colleagues.

EXHALE

Some of our racialized experiences inside the workplace have, for better or worse, shaped how we see ourselves. While the whole Kerry situation was taking place, I was blaming myself for this abuse. I went down the rabbit hole, thinking I had somehow brought this on myself. I'd say, *If only I had just stayed in Los Angeles, this never would have happened.* I kept thinking that I could've handled this differently, I could've avoided this pain. I had so much guilt.

First off, that was an unhealthy way to address and unpack my pain. After everything that happened, I had to actively start seeing myself in a new way, as someone who wasn't defined by my workplace scars. Ruminating on a past that you can't control can distract you from what healing you can do. I chose to address my pain so that I could take better control of my future. By learning to do that, I slowly started to release myself from any guilt.

In some ways, the act of finally acknowledging that Kerry was racially abusing me forced me to seek out the deeper healing I needed. The process of revisiting that painful time in my career meant that I finally gave myself permission to acknowledge all the previous racialized workplace heartbreaks that I had dug a grave for and had tried to forget about. There comes a time when, if we choose ourselves, we have to confront those ghosts so we can be free of them.

Addressing our pain doesn't have to be scary; it can lead to liberation. My prayer for you is that you begin to address your pain so you don't have to feel stifled.

Time to Unpack and Reassess

1. What does healing look like to you?
2. What has been your internal dialogue when it comes to addressing your pain?
3. Who were you before this racialized workplace experience, and who are you now?
4. Do you find it hard to trust your colleagues? Why?
5. How would you like your colleagues or manager to create psychological safety for you?
6. What does a good workplace look like to you?
7. What restoration agreements would you need to feel safe at work?
8. Write one or two restoration agreements that you would like to discuss with your manager and/or colleagues.

Chapter 3

HEALING FOR MY SOUL

I've watched my dreams get broken
In you I hope again!

—Tauren Wells, "Hills and Valleys"

As I began my healing journey, I started by leaning on my faith. Christianity had always been a source of strength for me in good times and in bad. When I began to think about what healing would look like for me, it was a no-brainer to start with the form that I knew most about, healing through prayer.

Before I go on, I want to put this disclaimer out to you: In this book we will uncover many different ways to heal from our racialized workplace trauma. For some of you, you might want to lean on your religion. And if you don't practice in the same manner as I do, or if you lean more toward the agnostic side of the house, I ask that you still go ahead and read this chapter to the end. I believe there is something in this section for everyone; it's always better to know all the tools that are available for your tool kit, even if you end up only using certain ones going forward. And I include various religions and perspectives, not just my own. This book is all about inclusion. Now, with that said, part of my tool kit included a faith practice, and I look forward to sharing more about that with you.

Racism isn't new. It's just that for so long, many white people would never acknowledge it, and we didn't always have the language to describe our pain related to racial injustice in the workplace. Racism has been living its best life since white people started forcing Indigenous people from their lands, and this was happening long before this nation's founding. For centuries, racism has violently devastated people across all communities of color. As I sit here and write, I can't help but think about all the migrant children who were detained at the border and trapped inside cages, because racism won over humanity during the Trump administration. I often think about the racial trauma those children will grow up with, and my hope is that by the time they become our age we will have resources and reparations to make their years of trauma a little more bearable.

Racial trauma isn't something you can easily outgrow. I remember the first time I was called a racial slur. I was twelve years old. A white child called me a "tar baby." There are a lot of things I don't remember about being twelve, but the phrase "tar baby" has been etched in my brain, and I can't forget how it made me feel—heck, how it still makes me feel! It's infuriating that so many white people have allowed racism to breathe as long as it has, while it suffocates the rest of us. Maya Angelou said, "Hate, it has caused a lot of problems in the world, but not solved one yet."

We do need to consider intergenerational trauma—and intergenerational healing. Healing ourselves can help the next generation breathe easier. And if we don't take control of our narrative, if we don't find tools to heal, then we can't pass any tools on to the next generation. While the nation continues its work during each era of racial reckoning, we can also create space for ourselves to find wholeness within and to help protect those who will enter our workplaces in the future.

LABELS

Labels, labels, labels—and I'm not talking about designer brands. Has anyone ever labeled you something that didn't sit well with you? For example, when Bernadine (Angela Bassett) burned up her husband's things in the front yard in *Waiting to Exhale*, some men might have labeled her "crazy." But in fact, she wasn't crazy; Bernadine was hurt. Or, as another example, too often when a new mother was experiencing depression (before we had the term "postpartum depression"), many folks in our communities would dismiss her as crazy.

I think this is one of the reasons the angry Black woman trope is so prevalent. It's easier for someone to call us "angry" or "crazy" than to engage in a real dialogue. And perhaps this crazy label is just additional baggage, keeping many women of color from finding our healing. Maybe fear of that label is why so many people of color avoid seeking the help we need. This ridiculous narrative that only crazy people get help continues to get passed on from one generation to another. Do you want to know what *is* crazy? Saying dismissive stuff like that! I think back to every time I've heard an elder say, "She ain't right in the head no more." But did anyone ever ask her what healing looks like for her?

Allow yourself to think about how many Black women and other women of color went to their graves labeled crazy, when probably all they needed was some healing from their pain. The pain of being isolated, overlooked, never promoted, and without support. Not to mention all the other heartbreaks we experience in life. I write this book in remembrance of all our sisters who died with trauma in their bodies, who were never able to be right within. I don't want another one of us going to our grave labeled anything other than "free."

FAITH BASED

Trauma and pain are two words that communities of color know all too well. Many of us are descendants of enslaved people, the grandchildren of those detained in Japanese internment camps, or those who mourn the genocide of fellow Indigenous people. One common theme that each community shares is a belief in a higher power. They knew there had to be something guiding them that was bigger than themselves. Some might call that higher power Buddha, the ancestors, or Jesus Christ. Many people across faiths have found that they needed religion to help them get up each morning and believe in a better future. Octavia Butler once said, "Religion kept some of my ancestors alive, because it was all they had." For many of our ancestors, I am glad they had something other than a life filled with loss and pain to believe in.

For me, my anchor has always been in my Christian faith. I've been going to church as long as I have been living. And, in all honesty, when it comes to the trauma I've experienced in my life, as the elders would say, "If it had not been for the Lord on my side, where would I be?" Chile, I am just happy I am in a peaceful state of mind on most days. And when it comes to the healing I've experienced in my life, God has been my Robitussin. Can I get an amen? I have to remember to try to keep it light during certain parts of this book because I know healing can be painful. And sometimes we have to learn to laugh to keep from crying. But, if you find that you need a good cry, crying is allowed too.

Just like church, prayer has been part of my life ever since I learned as a child, "As you lay me down to sleep, I pray dear Lord my soul you'll keep. If I die before I wake, I pray dear Lord, my soul you'll take." At an early age, I learned that prayer was the lifeline to a possible solution whenever I was sick or in need. All I had to do was call God up and tell him what I needed. That was the recipe, and those were the lyrics to the songs we would sing on Sundays. I think back to the days when preachers would ask if anyone required prayer, and they would invite folks up to the altar. I fondly remember the laundry list of sicknesses and diseases that would roll off the preacher's tongue, almost like *The Price Is Right*. If you're dealing with that sugar (diabetes), *come on down*. If your (blood) pressure is high, *come on down*. If you're having marriage issues, *y'all come on down*.

I was always that kid sitting in my chair wondering who was coming down for what. Of course, that was nothing but grown folks' business! Yet, there was one thing I never heard the preacher say . . . *come on down* if you need healing from a mental illness or racial trauma. I imagine the entire church would run down the aisles, and no one would be left to play the organ. My point is, I started to wonder why mental health wasn't discussed in the church, yet being healed or receiving your healing is always a topic of conversation, specifically, in the Black church. Did we not believe that God could heal anything? Or perhaps would acknowledging our need to heal from racial trauma open up a lot of wounds that Black people weren't ready to address?

I believe we can use a faith-based approach to healing. I believe healing should be broken down into three parts: body, mind, and spirit. But unfortunately, not many churches look at healing in the same way. Although I am happy to report churches like Faithful Central Bible Church, in Inglewood, California, has an entire counseling center as part of their church resources. As that church describes, "They provide counseling services by a trained staff of professionals who integrate theology and psychological and educational techniques." Just think about how transformative it would be to include a trained counselor or therapist on the pastoral staff. I believe many pastors (though well-intentioned) do their church members a disservice by thinking they alone can counsel every member to health. Don't get me wrong, Jesus is still on the main line; I just think he gave us additional resources to tap into as well.

A FANTASTIC VOYAGE

Let's explore the history of healing as it relates to the church. Many of the interviews that you will read later in this chapter are with faith leaders who have a fresh perspective on healing.

With that said, if you have a more agnostic view, I hope that you, too, will be able to pull some gems from this chapter and consider pieces that might apply to your healing path. My road to healing included a spiritual approach, along with other techniques.

I am surprised more Black churches don't talk about the importance of mental hygiene as it relates to racialized trauma. According to the *Encyclopedia Britannica*, mental hygiene is "the science of maintaining mental health and preventing the development of psychosis, neurosis, or other mental disorders." I know what you might be thinking: Is racial trauma a mental disorder? I don't know the clinical answer to that, but when I experienced traumatic race-related situations in the workplace, it led to the deterioration of my mental health. The trauma I was experiencing manifested in the form of panic attacks, anxiety, and depression. I should note that the American Psychological Association refers to racial trauma in this way: "Many ethnic and racial groups experience higher rates of post-traumatic stress disorder (PTSD) as compared to White Americans. One explanation for this is the experience of racism, which can itself be traumatic." According to the Mayo Clinic, PTSD "is a mental health condition that's triggered by a terrifying event—either experiencing it or witnessing it. Symptoms may include flashbacks, nightmares and severe anxiety, as well as uncontrollable thoughts about the event." I am not certified in anything other than being a Black woman, but what I do know without a shadow of a doubt is that racial trauma ain't healthy for any of us.

Kelly Price sings, "Take away this pain and misery / 'Cause God, I just can't do this by myself / I need help." It's such a profound line because, at the crux of it, she's saying we can't heal alone. But before anything, we first have to admit: we are in pain. We need the right tools to improve ourselves, yet we shouldn't feel shame for seeking out our own healing. If we go back to the Old Testament, there were plenty of people in the Bible who experienced pain and received healing from trauma, even some that happened in the workplace. I want to share two examples for those who might not yet grasp where I'm going with this. Remember, we are on a fantastic voyage.

First, let's take a look at one of the most popular characters in the Bible, David. In the book of Psalms, 55:2–3 in the New International Version (NIV), he writes, "My thoughts trouble me, and I am distraught because of what my enemy is saying, because of the threats of the wicked; for they bring down suffering on me and assail me in their anger." David continues to talk about his mental state in verses 4 through 7:

> *My heart is in anguish within me;*
> *the terrors of death have fallen on me.*
> *Fear and trembling have beset me;*
> *horror has overwhelmed me.*
> *I said, "Oh, that I had the wings of a dove!*
> *I would fly away and be at rest.*
> *I would flee far away*
> *and stay in the desert.*

Yo, David was pleading for some peace in his situation. It's clear to me that he was experiencing some sort of trauma. Now, I am going to take some liberties here with this verse.

Think about it in a career context. Suppose the enemy he is referring to is a toxic manager or colleague. Many of us have probably been in David's shoes. Have you ever been so overwhelmed by a workplace experience that you just wanted to throw up the deuces and leave it all? I know you can't see me, but I am raising my hand too. I was dealing with a white colleague who was making the workplace unbearable. And it wasn't just that she was a bully, but that there was racialized bullying taking place.

At first, I tried to tell myself she didn't mean any harm, because you know our go-to button isn't calling someone racist. It's the last thing we want to call it. The horrible treatment I received, while everyone watched, escalated to the point of no return. I would daydream like David and wish I could fly off to somewhere other than my office. All I had to show for the struggle were crushed dreams and lots of anxiety, and my enemy continued to live her best life, despite the devastation she had left in mine. Oh, and I know what you Bible scholars might be thinking. *Minda, don't you remember that other verse, "Be anxious for nothing"?* Yes, but God never said we wouldn't ever be anxious. He knew life would bring about those feelings. But the Bible does say, "The peace of God, which surpasses all understanding, will guard your hearts and minds through Christ Jesus." Meaning, we are all in need of a little peace. You can't get through the anxiety without finding your remedy to peace. Peace is available to all of us. Peace for you might be found by working out, by talking through your situation with a friend, or through counseling from a faith-based practitioner. The bottom line is, it's hard to thrive when you have no peace!

Before I move on, we are going to talk about a lot of topics related to healing. I realize not every person reading or listening to this book believes in the same spiritual tenets, but I hope you will indulge me a bit while I create my thesis. There is no one way to heal, and I hope we are all mature enough to read and educate ourselves on those various routes. The next example of biblical pain comes from the story of Joseph. The story goes a little something like this: Joseph was working at his day job while thinking about his side hustle, and his boss's wife, I think her name might have been Karen, kept trying to holler at him. He did his best to avoid her, but she was persistent. He finally got the nerve to have a courageous conversation with Karen and let her know he wasn't going to ruin his job; he told her to fall back. She didn't like that and called 911 and accused him of attacking her. Her husband was furious because he had promoted Joseph and felt betrayed, even though his wife was lying. Long story short, Joseph got thrown in jail. I must say, Joseph already had a tumultuous childhood, and this situation probably felt like a blow just when he thought he was moving up the ladder. Some of us aren't that different from Joseph. Many of us are working hard, minding our business, when all of a sudden someone comes and touches our hair, butchers our name, or just flat out says a joke that is racially motivated and everyone is laughing but you. It's almost like we've come to expect to be racially profiled or aggressed in the workplace by white people because it happens so often, which is no way to live our lives. It's hard to keep good mental hygiene when you're always in a state of trauma.

I tell you the story of Joseph because there is something very significant about it. He experienced sexual harassment and racial trauma. In the Bible story, it talks of his "workplace Karen" calling him a racial slur. When she tells her side of the story, she says, "This Hebrew." So clearly those were fighting words. This story also reminds me of the now infamous 2020 Central Park incident of a Caucasian woman, Amy Cooper, calling 911 on a Black man named Christian Cooper because he asked her to put her dog on a leash. In the video, Amy made it very clear that he was a "Black man." It's unfortunate that this desperate white-woman playbook still exists, but you know what equally still exists? Racial trauma. Albeit, no media outlet discussed how this racialized situation will leave a lasting impact on Christian Cooper's mental wellness, and how it will affect how he shows up at work, or any other place for that matter. This situation happened during one of the most racialized periods in my life, where unarmed Black men and women were being murdered left and right during a global pandemic. Christian was one of the "lucky" ones, in that he survived, yet can you imagine how much trauma he might be dealing with today? We shouldn't have to live in racial terror. Addressing our need to heal might be one step forward.

I'm telling you these Bible stories in part to say that racism and trauma aren't new, and in part to say that some of these stories can validate our experiences. As we'll see, faith can also help lead us out of our trauma. If you find comfort in reading the Bible, perhaps it helps to know that two people who God favored were greeted with trauma in their lives, but when they sought out healing and prayer they were able to find a way out. Sometimes we just need to know that we aren't alone, and that others found healing on their journey as well. That might even encourage you to seek it out too. I believe these stories were intentionally placed in the Bible to remind us that sadness might last for a night, but joy can come in the morning with the right tools in our life. And we will talk more about those tools as we work through this book.

NO, I AM NOT OKAY

As you dig deeper into this book, I will share many stories of racialized experiences during my career that caused me a lot of pain. Being the only Black woman at work, I felt like I was constantly walking on eggshells, because I didn't want to come across as too Black, aggressive, or hostile. It's really hard to do your job and be worried about how everyone else perceives you. The funny thing is, I doubt any of my colleagues ever wondered if they were being too white. Maybe if they had worried about their role in workplace racism, they would have shown up by treating me a little bit better. As I began to think about what healing might look like for me to be free of this oppressive system, I started to realize that even though my colleagues might have caused my trauma, ultimately, it was my decision if I was going to stay in that trauma. I realized that I didn't want to live in fear, panic, and anxiety every day at work. There was no way I could change them, but I could definitely choose to be right within. If I was being devalued by others, I at least had to be sure that I still valued myself. I deserved that much.

For so long, I used to tell myself to suck it up when certain racialized experiences would happen to me at work. I would tell myself, *Well, Minda, at least you aren't getting whipped on a plantation.* Or, *At least you're not being branded for trying to run away from work.* Or, *Your trauma isn't nearly as bad as your ancestors', so just keep doing your job.* I am embarrassed to admit to you that I was minimizing my workplace trauma and comparing it to the working conditions of the enslaved. I started to believe the white narratives we hear so often, like, "It's better now than it was back then," when those sayings seemed to suggest that with the passage of time, things will somehow naturally get better. I remember being at a client lunch at an exclusive club when my white client said, "I don't understand why you people get so worked up over Donald Trump. You did have a Black president. Times have changed a lot—be happy." Thank God, at that time I had a little healing in my body, because otherwise those words probably would have drained me for days just trying to dissect what he was really trying to get at. I hate hearing racialized comments like that. Yes, we have come a mighty long way. Yet while the workplaces look a little different, Black people are still experiencing a lot of the same demeaning treatment, facing ignorance and hurtful words day in and day out. The sad and ugly truth is that white people are still trying to minimize our pain, sometimes by pretending racism was solved by the country having a Black president.

I started to get tired of sweeping all of these racial grievances under the rug. I mean, at what point are we going to hold these people and the workplaces accountable for the trauma we encounter when we just want to do the best work of our careers, and they keep making it harder due to the color of our skin? I was no longer satisfied with finding that I could somewhat withstand this treatment. I wanted to thrive at work, not just survive. At this point in my life, I didn't know where I could go for help. I didn't even consider therapy back then. I only had one idea of what healing could look like for me, and so I decided to explore a faith-based approach.

I knew that these feelings were not healthy for me. I began to invest in myself and stop centering bad behavior in the workplace. This is when I started to feverishly ask God for some help, not just to get more money and a promotion, but to heal my mind and my achy-breaky heart from all of these racialized workplace experiences. I knew they were starting to become overwhelming. I started reading scriptures daily and speaking affirmations I had learned from Bill Winston, who is the pastor at Living Word Christian Center in Forest Park, Illinois. Pastor Bill had all of these prayers on his website that I would recite daily. And I still recite them. Ain't nothing changed but the day; these prayers are part of my healing tool kit.

A BRAND NEW KINDA FREE

When I was at the lowest point in my career life, I did a lot of praying. I was searching for some peace of mind. Not just peace from my toxic work environment—I needed a spiritual transformation as well.

According to the Pew Research Center, nearly 79 percent of African Americans identify as Christian. Yet I have lived enough life to know that intersectionality is essential regarding our beliefs. The Christian faith isn't the only religion that believes in healing. Take, as just one example, Tibetan Buddhists. Many believe that one's mind has the power to manifest sickness and health. While writing *Right Within*, I interviewed women of color who are leaders in their faiths, from Christianity to Buddhism to Islam. I wanted to be intentional in creating space for interfaith dialogue around healing. I asked these leaders questions related to healing and the role our faith should or could play as women of color healing from racialized work trauma. You will find that, no matter your preferred belief system, there are some common themes throughout the interviews. Additionally, they provide some unconventional perspectives we can use to counter any dismissive language we've faced in our communities growing up, which might have kept us from seeking the spiritual help we need. I have no doubt this is where you will start to highlight and take notes like it's nobody's business.

Remember when I asked you what does healing mean to you? I thought it was only fair to ask that question of the amazing women who took time out of their schedules to talk with me about healing. I first spoke with my mom, Marchet Harts. She is a minister at City of God Church in Rock Falls, Illinois. My mom talked about healing in this way: "Healing can take a long time or can happen instantaneously. And healing looks different for everyone. Jesus healed people in a variety of ways—there is no one way to achieve healing. Healing also takes work and can be a messy process, yet a rewarding one." I then made my way to my aunt Kasey Whitney; she is on the pastoral staff at Faithful Central Bible Church in Inglewood, California, and she described healing as "a layered onion. We have to start unpeeling the layers to understand how we need to heal, one layer at a time. Healing has to be tailor-made to the individual based on the individual's needs—that might require a group, one-on-one, or time alone, depending on their season of life."

My next stop on my healing listening tour was with Vashti McKenzie, a bishop of the African Methodist Episcopal Church, and she said, "The process in which one can be made whole is not always about getting back to where you were but moving onto a place where you're whole. Healing is about getting better." I spoke with Reverend Yolanda M. Norton, the H. Eugene Farlough professor of Black church studies at San Francisco Theological Seminary. She said that healing is "retrieving something about your most authentic self that has been lost due to situational or persistent trauma." As you can see, there are some common themes among their answers: that healing is a process that is individualized and that is about moving forward toward wholeness and authenticity. As I continued to ruminate on the wise words being quoted by these women of God, I started to wonder what an interfaith definition of healing from racial trauma might look like.

I reached out to Angelica Lindsey-Ali, also known as the Village Auntie, a leading voice for Muslim women. She said, "A good healer, in my eyes, is one that doesn't pre-scribe medicine, necessarily, but one who teaches or reminds the afflicted how to heal themselves. We are all born with the ability to repair and heal those parts of ourselves, but it is dif-ficult to have complete healing without others' aid." I didn't want to stop there, so I reached out to Bronwyn Morgan, a meditation coach and Reiki practitioner who founded Bliss in Me Meditation. I asked Morgan, a practicing Buddhist, what healing meant for her. She said, "Healing is a process in which we shed beliefs, mindsets, and attachments to the created self that keep us attached to the past. We then replace them with awareness and present mindedness, which are in alignment with our true nature. Our true nature is not disturbed by the past." And as you can see, healing isn't reserved for Christians only; it is available to all of us. Clearly, there are common beliefs in our abilities to heal ourselves, let go, and become free of our baggage.

WHERE I WANT TO BE

I must admit to you that, for many years, I didn't talk to anyone about my racial trauma in the workplace, because I was under the impression that this was just the way the workplace works for Black and Brown women. I hadn't given myself permission to explore normalizing a workplace that doesn't oppress women of color. I mean, wow, talk about creating an equitable workplace, one that doesn't oppress women of color every day? Now that is the job I want to sign up for. As I explored healing and asking God for guidance, I began to uncover that I didn't have to settle for mediocre. And I didn't have to settle for trauma that I didn't cause. When you begin to heal your mind, you also start to realize that you don't have to stay in an oppressive work environment. You can start to strategize and find a new place where you can be free.

As I was starting my journey toward healing from racial workplace trauma, I had a conversation with my dad, Larry Harts, who is the lead pastor at City of God in Rock Falls, Illinois. I asked him how he views healing from workplace trauma for women of color. He told me, "Minda, racial challenges can become your motivator toward your success, not your demise. Your former pitfalls do not dictate your future successes. The past negative experiences afford your inner warrior the opportunity to spring forth to fight for righteousness for yourself and for others. You were built to win!" He saw these racialized experiences as a possible devastation, but also as our greatest motivator for change. If we start to address our racialized pain, we are also helping to motivate those who might be in a more vulnerable situation than us. Meaning that our healing will help us and others, and that reflects Jesus's ministry.

Now I know what you're thinking. *He is your dad, Minda. He is supposed to tell you this.* But I asked him what advice he'd give to women in his congregation who suffer from racialized trauma. He said, "When we begin to talk about racial trauma, it is easy for people, mainly white people, to say, 'Why don't you just let it go, get over it?' Women of color realize that it is not that easy. When you have worked so hard to attain your position in the workplace, all to see it crushed and demolished right in front you, it is devastating. Most women of color have not experienced this just one time, but several times during their careers. So now, at the point of hopelessness and even consideration of giving up, you need to take a breath and decide that this is the time to rebuild. You will not give in to indignation and ridicule."

After we hung up the phone that day, he called me back to drop one last gem. Pastor Larry said, "It is very important for you to realize who you are, and the inherent awesome strength that dwells on the inside of you. If you count on someone else to provide you with an evaluation of your character, potential, and abilities, then you will always be enslaved to their ideologies and untruths. Keep in mind, these people are ignorant when it comes to your destiny in life, therefore they are not qualified to dictate it. Racial trauma goes way beyond the workplace. It touches every aspect of your life." This conversation was very special to me, because it was the first time that I had talked about my trauma with my dad. And in that moment, I realized that healing doesn't have to be done alone. I can be vulnerable and share my healing journey so that others can be free as well.

HEALING AIN'T EASY

After having that conversation with my dad, I wanted to take it a step further and ask Pastor Kasey and Reverend Yolanda their thoughts on being a woman of color and how it can be hard for us to take that first step to admit to ourselves that we have been harmed racially inside the workplace. Because, let's be honest, many of us haven't even acknowledged that our workplaces have caused us harm. Pastor Kasey said, "There has been a stigma that has been placed around therapy or asking for help. The narrative being: the only place you can get help is in the church. As a culture, we've learned to judge others. It's easier just to label someone instead of investigating what might be causing the need to heal. We've passed down the advice of 'Suck it up and be strong.' Or 'Therapy is only for white people.' Healing is crucial so you can break down what's going on in your life and allow yourself to be built up—yet we haven't been taught that."

Pastor Kasey is right on the money. We have to normalize conversations around healing in a real way. Reverend Yolanda explained, "Trauma is all we know—we don't know what it feels like not to have trauma surrounding us. Only a particular group of people in this country have been allowed to name their trauma. And in the Black community naming our trauma has been equated as a weakness." I don't know about you, but I definitely feel like we are being taken to church right now. When I first started to explore the depth of my pain, I felt shame that I wasn't strong enough to push past these experiences. After all, that is what many of us have been told to do. But I am here to tell you, we have the option to be right within, and our lives depend on it. Our mental health depends on it.

Like I have mentioned before, healing is not a one-time event but a daily practice. It's important to know that you deserve to heal from trauma, and important to acknowledge that trauma should never have been inflicted upon you in the first place. Please don't ever question if you deserve to be treated with dignity at work. During my conversations with Bronwyn Morgan, Angelica Lindsey-Ali, and Pastor Marchet, we explored the consequences of Black women not permitting themselves to heal. You best believe there will be some consequences if we continue on this racialized path without any tools at our disposal.

Morgan said, "We will continue to carry a history of hurts that block our ability to be fully ourselves. By not giving ourselves space and the permission to heal, we drag everything that's happened as if it is happening each moment that we march forward. This perspective often creates an environment for the same types of experiences to occur again and again. We are not alone or unique to this, but we've carried deep burdens from generation to generation. We can put down the past and be open and ready to lead, love, and transform."

Lindsey-Ali added her perspective: "When we don't give ourselves space to repair, rebuild, and replenish, the entire foundation of society suffers. We are the prototypes, the generators, the nourishers, the leaders. Our society may not give us our rightful due in the title, but our function is clear. Black women and other women of color are the axis around which so much of our good culture spins. When we deny ourselves permission and space to heal, we implode and cause serious harm, not only to ourselves but also to the community. And these ailments are a direct result of the psychic violence and emotional terror that comes when access to healing is removed or impeded."

When I was finishing the interview with my mom, she closed our conversation by adding, "We have the opportunity to turn our pain into a cause. Healing isn't always just for us. Our healing can help heal others too. And if we isolate too long, our isolation might create more pain, and you risk becoming emotionally sicker."

Let's keep it real for a second: We know what our lives feel like without healing, so what could they look and feel like with it? With all of the racialized experiences both inside and outside the workplace, we can't afford not to at least try to explore living a life that is less traumatized. So many people are waiting on us to heal so they can heal too.

EVERYONE HAS A ROLE TO PLAY

Many of us grew up in church, and we might still attend church in some way, shape, or form. Even though the church hasn't always leaned into healing from racial trauma in the past, I feel like there is a role the church can currently play for women of color in the workplace. I mean, think about how many women of color attend church. This is a missed opportunity to add an additional layer of coverage and allyship in supporting them.

Initially, I felt weird challenging the church or questioning its role in our healing from racialized trauma. But then I thought, *Let me ask the experts, so no one thinks I am being blasphemous.* Bishop Vashti told me this: "The church should be creating safe spaces for women of color and Black women to share how they feel. A place where they can verbalize their experiences of racial and gender trauma without judgment. Part of the church's role should be respecting her humanity by not labeling a woman who has been harmed by the disease of racism. The church talks a lot about trouble, but not enough about trauma. Trouble runs through your life; trauma takes a long walk."

Reverend Yolanda believes "the church must understand that healing is wellness. This stigma around therapy is part of the patriarchy. Treatment is part of our wellness and not our illness. God has given us tools and blessed not just parishioners with gifts, but also others with the gift of grace to listen and reflect. God can heal you on a couch too. Receiving additional help outside of the church from others should be viewed as tapping into another spiritual discipline."

Last but not least, Pastor Marchet said, "We need to learn to hear people out. Allow women to find the right church and team of people who will honor their feelings and then let them talk about their pain. The church shouldn't be a place where women have to question themselves or their pain."

I get goosebumps just thinking about the role the church can play, now and in the future, as it relates to supporting women of color on their journey to healing, without judgment. Often, women of color are not able to talk about their pain without judgment, so it would be awesome if the church could aid in our healing process.

BATTERIES NOT INCLUDED

As I continued to think about my healing journey, it took me a long while to forgive those in the workplace who had harmed me. Their harm caused me a lot of damage. Even though I haven't forgotten about that, I can honestly say I forgive every last person who caused me racialized harm, even when none of them ever apologized for it. I had to make a choice to forgive myself. Meaning, I had to stop blaming myself for what they did to me. I blamed myself for not standing up and not holding my colleagues accountable. I realize that not everyone will choose to forgive; nor do you have to. But I did want to explore the idea of forgiveness as something that can be tied to our healing.

Angelica Lindsey-Ali said, "To forgive is to release the psychological hold that another person or entity has on our spirit. But it does not mean that we are required to forget the wrongdoing in the first place. Forgiveness allows a person to move freely, with the benefit of soft barriers erected to protect the heart from further damage. Forgiveness does not breed bitterness, but it should create a ripe setting for forbearance and insight."

Bronwyn Morgan explained that we can seek "forgiveness of oneself and those who have hurt us. Forgiveness isn't about willingly allowing others to damage us; it's about knowing that people are where they are on their journey and karmic energy. Irritation, fear, sadness, shame, and blame are all manifestations of anger. As Buddha states, 'Holding on to anger is like grasping a hot coal with the intent of throwing it at someone else; you are the one who gets burned.' We can put down the anger, but we must address that it's there and acknowledge what we've been feeling to expose it fully. Pain from this type of trauma can manifest in the body and create both physical and mental illness."

I had to ask Bishop Vashti her thoughts on forgiveness, and she said, "Withholding forgiveness hurts more for the person who has been traumatized. If one doesn't forgive, it could result in the traumatization of others. Part of forgiveness is refusing to be the victim. The Bible states, 'The thief comes to kill, steal, and destroy.' If we don't allow ourselves to forgive, it will break into our bodies in other ways."

As you start to uncover what healing looks like for you, I hope that you will explore what forgiveness might look like as well. Though I realize some of us might not be ready to forgive just yet.

Now, I don't want you to forget why we are here. This journey is about you learning how to become right within. So please think about the advice given, because you can start to activate your healing at any time. I enjoyed being able to ask these faith leaders and healers about their perspectives. One response that has stayed with me came from my mom. During our interview, she said, "If we don't at least try and heal, we are just running from our pain, and we enter into a cycle of trauma." And that's the last thing I want for you—to be trapped in a cycle of traumatic hell, where your pain is being played over and over again on a loop. I believe God wants us to heal, because it was never his will for us to experience this harm in the first place.

NOT OLD-TIME RELIGION

As I began to remember my past thoughts around healing and faith, I thought about how far I have come since those initial inquiries many years ago. Healing isn't just for the folks in the Old and New Testament; healing can happen right now, today. Most importantly, healing can happen if you are open to it. I had a conversation with Shanika Hart (no relation), a licensed master social worker and the co-pastor, with her husband Pastor Kenneth Hart, of a church I attend in Harlem, New York, called the Gathering Harlem. I asked Shanika Hart a series of questions right after the George Floyd and Breonna Taylor murders, because I was triggered by some of my past trauma, seeing these racialized experiences of people who look like me on my television screen.

I asked Hart if there were any Bible stories or scriptures that have helped her when dealing with racism in the workplace, because she is a Black woman just like me. She said, "When it comes to scriptures that are healing to my heart and mind amidst racist encounters, there are several verses that can be applied when dealing with racism in the workplace. At this moment though, what comes up for me are verses like Isaiah 10:1–2: 'Woe to those who make unjust laws, to those who issue oppressive decrees, to deprive the poor of their rights and withhold justice from the oppressed of my people, making widows their prey and robbing the fatherless.' And Psalm 89:14: 'Righteousness and justice are the foundation of your throne; steadfast love and faithfulness go before you.'"

She said, "In both of these verses, I am reminded that the Lord cares about injustices, and, to be more specific, those committed against me or those who I love. His righteous anger is personalized to each one of us!

"Racism reveals the fact that we live in a fallen world, where someone can be marginalized and negatively targeted because of the color of their skin. What has been most grounding is the fact that the Bible was written from the lens of the oppressed, not of those in power, so that means that the Lord understands when I burn in anger due to the injustices done against me. Further, one of the names of God is El Roi, which means 'God sees me.' I don't have to explain the sadness and anger that I am filled with when I am made to feel like I am anything less than the image bearer of Christ, and worthy of dignity. And I have confidence that because the Lord hates white supremacy, sees my pain, and loves me, that he will guard my heart and mind and be my defense under those circumstances. And he will give me the agency, by way of his spirit, to exercise discernment and to speak truth to power when possible."

Outside of Hart being a mental health practitioner, she is also a faith leader, and I had to ask her, as a pastor who has a large majority of women of color in her congregation, what advice she would give another Black woman on how the church can help her heal from racial trauma. She responded, "Since the time of chattel slavery, throughout the Jim Crow South and the years that followed, Black people have drawn strength and healing from communal spaces with each other. Whether it was singing Negro spirituals or sharing stories of trials or triumph, we were all that we had sometimes, and between community and the Lord, quite frankly, that's just what we needed. Today, it's no different, sis. The church presents an ideal opportunity for healing in spaces with people who may or may not look like you but who, more times than not, believe as you do in the power of Jesus. And Jesus speaks hope and healing into those moments. But at times we might not remember how to heal, so having a community of like-minded believers who can remind us of Jesus's heart for the marginalized is essential.

"It is equally important for us to be reminded how the gospel of Jesus transforms every situation. In the case of racism—knowing that racism is a sin that Jesus died for. Racism is something that breaks his heart and is against his will, because it seeks to tear down the very people that Jesus seeks to uphold. But Jesus's power was proven to be greater than that of racism because he defeated sin, death, and Satan on the cross, and he will return for his church one day, where we will live in perfect fellowship with him—where racism will have no place and where, in our glorified bodies, we will radiate beautifully, in all hues, just as we were created to on earth."

Whew . . . can I get an amen? Just being able to glean all of these amazing gems from other Black and Brown women has done my soul good. These words have even helped me think about healing in an entirely new context. As someone who has healed from some racialized work trauma, and who is still working my way through some other events, one thing I know to be true is that healing is necessary; you just have to decide which tools you want to use to get there.

THE DOORS OF THE CHURCH ARE OPEN

For some of you who aren't as churchy as me, I still pray that you found something in those conversations that made you think about your healing a little differently. And perhaps you might even add components of faith-based strategies on your path toward being whole. Please just remember that healing takes time. Even if you are racially aggressed again, don't let anyone get in the way of your chance to continue on your healing journey, because healing isn't just for you. Pastor Kasey said, "Sometimes, people give up on their healing too soon. And the people who love us or want to get to know us better never get to experience the real you. And most importantly, you don't get to be the best you. You will suffer in your self-esteem, and unrealistic expectations of other people could potentially torment you. You will end up as sick as your secrets. Meaning, if we keep the pain a secret, it only hurts us in the end." So whether you seek help from the church, therapy, family, or friends, I hope you don't suffer in silence any longer.

Oh, and I wanted to follow up with telling you more about Joseph's story. I think it could be helpful as you continue in your career. Joseph went through hell and back, but he eventually received some healing and peace. His story didn't end with him locked up abroad; he had a happy ending. Joseph ascended to the highest ranks of leadership. He found healing in his mind and body, and eventually in his career. The Bible says that Joseph received healing from his workplace trauma. He ended up naming his first son Manasseh, which means, "God has made me forget all my trouble" (Genesis 41:51). For someone to forget all of their troubles, I guarantee it took some hard work to get there. My guess is Joseph didn't heal in isolation, and neither should you.

Time to Unpack and Reassess

Each chapter will require a little something from you. For this chapter, that time is now. One exercise I would like to invite you to participate in is to ask yourself some of the same questions I asked our faith leaders, with one caveat—you have to make it personal. This reflection time only works when we are honest with ourselves. The time we spend together is not about facades or asking ourselves *What will people think?* Our healing has nothing to do with what other people might think. It's time we center ourselves. Let's get into it!

1. What does healing mean to you now?
2. Has there been a time in your career when you've experienced racial trauma that replays in your mind? Is it hard to admit? If yes, why?

3. If you were to consider pursuing a faith-based approach to your healing, what role would you like your religion to play in your healing journey?

4. Would forgiveness be a useful tool for the racial trauma you are considering for this exercise?

5. Is there a way to rewrite the story of your trauma, as a way to find strength or as an opportunity to make the path easier for the next woman of color?

6. What are the potential consequences of not pursuing a path to healing? Are there ways that your pain has started affecting those around you?

How did that exercise feel for you? I know it can be tough answering questions that might lead us to places we aren't ready to visit. But if not now, when? A spiritual approach, mixed with a few other healing tools, helped me along my journey. In the next chapter, we will explore therapy as a path to healing. Healing is an inside job; you just have to decide which tools you want to use. Healing is also a choice. It's one I can't and won't force on you, but I want you to know what is out there. Additionally, there are interfaith spaces that want to make themselves available to you that will hear you out. You can find some additional resources at the end of this book.

Chapter 4

TRYING TO BE RIGHT WITHIN

I've got some issues that nobody can see
And all of these emotions are pouring out of me
—Kid Cudi, "Soundtrack to My Life"

I n the previous chapter, I mentioned some of the stigma associated with therapy and mental wellness. Some folks want us to use church for our healing journey or nothing at all. In some of our communities, there's a projected shame toward those who decide to go to therapy. And God forbid you go to therapy and church at the same time—some would probably call that an abomination. There's this unwelcome narrative that the reason we're suffering is because we are not praying enough or do not have enough faith. And that is a narrative I can't get behind one bit.

You don't end up in *The Guinness Book of World Records* because you can pray and see a therapist simultaneously; it is possible for lots of people to do both. I believe we need various tools for our life, and therapy could be another tool you might consider using as you heal from racialized trauma. Again, I didn't write this book to dictate what healing should look like for you. I just want you to know what tools are available.

THE T-WORD

I realize I just said the T-word. Yep, therapy. I am not ashamed to say that therapy has helped me through many trying times in my career when I needed it the most. And treatment continues to be a support system I can rely on when dealing with racial aggressions that might come my way. And let me clear up a quick myth: racism doesn't stop because you've arrived at the table, or even if you've built your own table. I still deal with slights as a Black woman entrepreneur. Only now can I walk away or have a hard conversation without as high a penalty as I might have had in my former career. Therapy also helps me maintain a healthier state of mind, so I don't burn out on those triggering days. I go to therapy regularly, but that doesn't mean that I am experiencing a racialized trauma every day; I also use therapy as a form of maintenance. Sometimes we need our healing tools to make sure we don't relapse and to ensure that we can maintain what we have worked so hard to secure.

Before you decide whether therapy is for you, my only ask is that you hear me out. If you have never been, then you can't say it will never work, am I right? And one thing I have learned from living a little bit is never to say never. Or perhaps you've tried therapy and had a bad experience, and you have decided, *Oh, chile, never again.* I know that feeling is real too. But let's say you go to a new trendy restaurant that has fantastic reviews, but you end up with a stomachache later that evening. Would you then declare that you will never go out to dinner ever again? No, you would find another restaurant that suits your palate. Finding the right therapist is no different, so I hope you won't rule it out completely.

IN ALL HONESTY

I wasn't sure I was ready to write *Right Within*, to be honest. Because writing this book would require me to show you behind-the-scenes details of what some may call a very personal journey. I remember sitting at my desk in sunny California and feeling like life was smacking me all around. To be clear, yes, I had a good job, I lived in a lovely apartment in Beverly Hills, and I was dating two people at the same time. I can appreciate Jada Pinkett Smith more than she will ever know—God knows that was indeed an entanglement—but thankfully that is not the book I am writing (and don't ever plan to)!

Every weekend, I hung out with my girlfriends like we were on an episode of *Entourage*, eating at some of the best restaurants in Los Angeles and traveling to beaches and abroad. On the surface, my life was pretty damn good. The only issue was, I was about to turn thirty years old, and I felt trapped. I felt like I had no agency to flip the table and start over. I was questioning myself at every turn, and the abuse was at its peak in the workplace. I guess you could say I was in a work entanglement too. I was serving as interim director of a department while still doing my former role. On paper, it looked like a promotion, yet it wasn't—but it took me a minute to figure that part out. I eventually had to negotiate my worth to get an additional stipend because I was doing two or three jobs. And there was no end in sight.

To make matters worse, the person with the position before me left it in a bit of disarray, so I was called upon to fix it all. You know workplaces love to call Black women to the crime scene when things have gone astray. Why do you think Olivia Pope was called "the fixer"? This is also known as the glass-cliff phenomenon. Meaning, women tend to be promoted into positions of power when there is a work crisis or failure from someone in leadership. Yet wouldn't it be nice to receive the phone call we have been dreaming about that doesn't require fixing anything? But that is probably a matter for another book. I am sure you have your stories too.

At this time in my life, I realized that I was not right within. But I didn't have the words to articulate how I was feeling, and I certainly didn't want to tell anyone. Because, in my mind, I thought if I told someone about this feeling, they might say to me I'm tripping or ungrateful for all God had given me. And I lightweight felt like I might be tripping too. Here we go, back to questioning myself again! I shamed myself for thinking I might need some help, and I didn't even understand the help I needed. That's when I started to consider therapy as an option.

A ROAD TRIP

One weekend, I got up and decided I needed to get away. I found this oasis outside of Palm Springs, California. They had no Wi-Fi, no TV, and six bungalows, with a few natural hot-spring pools. The first time I went, I left town and told no one. I thought this mental-health break was either going to go well, or I'd end up at some Heaven's Gate cult kind of place and I'd be screwed. I said a prayer, like, *Lord, you know I need this me-cation. Please protect me.* I grabbed a bottle of wine, packed my bag, and drove down the highway until I reached my destination. Back then I didn't have Siri; I was on team BlackBerry. So all I had was this clunky Garmin GPS that I stuck to my dashboard that slid off every so often.

For three days, I reflected on my pain, but at the time I didn't realize it was racialized. My default thinking centered around me being the problem. *There must have been something wrong with me.* That is what a system of oppression is meant to do—make us feel like we did something to deserve this treatment. I started to think back to my first corporate job as an administrative assistant and how most of us were women of color. Management treated us terribly. And our supervisor was like Angelica from *Rugrats,* but all grown up. I started to have flashbacks of all of this inequity I had faced in the workplace and how often the pain that I was feeling had a racialized component. I started to see a theme: racism. I wasn't sure what all of this meant, but I knew I needed to do something.

SHRINKS

My entire life, I have watched white people on TV talk about their shrinks. I've seen them lying on all the couches, and not in the same way that Dave Chappelle put his feet on the couch when he played Rick James on *Chappelle's Show*. I started wondering if I might need to sit on somebody's couch too. There's this interesting narrative that Black folks don't do anything outside the box. We don't ski, we don't swim, we don't jump out of planes. And we don't do therapy. Folks out here probably thinking that Black people aren't living their best lives, that they don't take any risks. I guess I was part of the problem too, because I've thought this way, and I am Black. But of course, many of us do all of those activities. But the therapy part, that was a narrative I had started to believe. When I think back on it, I'd never heard any positive stories shared about therapy, nor was I exposed to Black women, in particular, who advocated going to therapy. No one I knew had ever admitted that they had gone to therapy. It seemed like it was something reserved for the white people on *Lifestyles of the Rich and Famous*.

Whenever I started to think about finding a therapist, I dismissed it, because I didn't know that Black people got that type of help. Yet, the older I get, the more I realize the reluctance behind therapy probably exists in communities of color due to stigma, judgment, and lack of cultural understanding. The fact that we are told that we have to be strong and push past our trauma is killing us softly.

In today's pop culture, we're now seeing people of color discussing mental health everywhere from comedy specials to scripted series. And that makes my heart smile, because the next generation won't have to be held captive by What Would Others Think Syndrome (WWOTS).

WWOTS

For me, I was part of the WWOTS camp. What would others think if they saw me walking into that building? I mean, it's right on Wilshire and Fairfax, one of the busiest intersections in Los Angeles. What would others think if they saw I was using my insurance this way? They were going to be talking about me in the HR office. And what would my family think? Because for some reason I felt like I needed their permission or something. I needed a therapist just to unpack my WWOTS bias, to get it out of my way. In reality, why should I care what anyone else thinks of me trying to achieve my authentic self and heal? Many of us would rather suffer in silence than become vulnerable and seek help, and I don't want that for you. Asking for help is a revolutionary act. And it's one that I don't think enough of us are using as a tool toward our healing.

My goal in this chapter isn't to convince you that therapy is the be-all and end-all to healing. You aren't some appliance that needs a new double-A battery and, boom, you're fixed. To be honest, it's not even about someone fixing you. Healing, in my opinion, is about you trying to get closer to your authentic self. So many of life's ills and disappointments have chipped away at who we are as women. Things like the salary gap and being overlooked for promotions, it's a lot of baggage to carry as women of color—and that is just the adult stuff. We haven't even talked about unpacking childhood trauma. Lord Jesus, help us!

I want to dispel some myths about therapy, because this book might be the only resource to give you the 411 and help you make an informed decision. I am going to share how I found a therapist and my experience sitting on my first couch. I also interviewed some of the top women of color therapists and got their take on therapy as an additional tool in our healing tool kit around racialized trauma in the workplace.

I have to admit to you that I almost didn't go to therapy because I thought it might be too expensive. When you're on the fence about something, it's easy to create a million excuses to talk yourself out of it. Then, one day, I overheard one of my colleagues tell someone else that she has great insurance and a low co-pay, and now she is set up to go to therapy weekly. Immediately, I thought that I probably have the same coverage, and the wheels in my head started turning. When I got home, I looked at my insurance plan, and therapy was covered. I got on the internet and combed through the list for in-network mental health providers.

WHATCHA LOOKING FOR?

Let me pause here. I didn't know fully what I was looking for in a therapist, but I did know two things: (1) she needed to be a woman and (2) a woman of color. No offense, but some of what I imagined I would be talking about was my job, and there was no way I was going to a white person who couldn't identify with what I was experiencing. I was already fragile, and the last thing I needed to hear was some white therapist telling me that Bob didn't mean any harm. I wanted a safe space where I could be honest and not center whiteness. That wasn't the couch I wanted to pay to sit on. After combing through the list, I found a woman whose practice was around the corner from my apartment. Jackpot.

Before we move on, let's talk about the steps you can take to find a therapist:

1. If you have insurance, start by assessing which therapists are considered in-network and the fees associated with finding a therapist who might be out of network. Also, if you don't have insurance, many therapists will work with you on a sliding scale. Don't count it out because you assume you can't afford therapy. You deserve healing.

2. Consider your needs. I shared with you that I had two nonnegotiables: the therapist needed to be a woman and a woman of color. My needs are not necessarily the same as yours, so please permit yourself to think through the type of therapist you might want to work with.

3. My therapist was a psychotherapist. Some are psychiatrists, counselors, or clinically licensed social workers. The main thing I would take into consideration is if the therapist is licensed or not. (Sidenote: you might even decide you want to work with a life coach, but I would also encourage you to see what certification they have.) Some therapists can prescribe medication, and others cannot. Every state has a Department of Consumer Affairs where you can verify if everything is on the up-and-up.

4. Check out the therapist's website. I hope that the therapist you choose has one. I want you to get to know

them before you sit on their couch. On their website, you can find out about their areas of expertise. That's imperative, especially if you want to talk to an expert about your workplace trauma—then, for example, you probably don't want to visit one who specializes in children's therapy.

5. Don't be shy. Think about the questions that you might want to ask before moving forward, and then call or email and ask those preliminary questions. Interview them like they are applying for a job. I mean, they kind of are! And don't assume you have the answers. Ask them what you need to know so you can move to an actual visit or keep looking for a therapist who suits your needs.

6. Lean on referrals if you still need help finding someone. It's okay to ask around. You can also use the website for the podcast *Therapy for Black Girls* as a resource, which has a list of providers.

I didn't know much about this process back then, but these are just some of the things I wish I had known. Start to think about what healing might look like for you and set reasonable expectations. A therapist cannot turn water into wine. They need you to help stomp the grapes, so that in partnership you both create and bottle the wine. As I told you before, healing takes work, and it can be painful. Beyoncé did tell us that "Pretty Hurts," and to get to the beauty, healing might hurt a bit. And it's hard to fix what you aren't willing to confront.

GUARD YOUR CHOICES

As I dug deeper down the benefits rabbit hole, I found out that my employer offered an employee assistance program, also known as an EAP. This meant they would cover a certain number of therapy sessions as a complimentary benefit. And the use of the EAP would be completely confidential. My employer offered three EAP therapy sessions. Now, I hate to admit this to you, but I thought, *This is perfect. All I need is three. Let me get these free sessions and move on with my life.* Little did I know, I would see that therapist for the next three years. I can laugh about it now because it's so funny that I thought I could solve my workplace troubles in three fifty-minute sessions. Kind of like some companies today, which believe they can solve four-hundred-plus years of systemic racism in the workplace in a week's worth of video conference calls.

After my third session, my therapist, Rashid, graciously made me aware that I needed more than three. I still felt a little shame around going in the first place, and I pushed back and said that I would come once a month. Who knew I had so much healing to do? Once I got out of my way and let Rashid do her job, I found therapy to be an act of self-love to help me pack lighter. I realized that I didn't have to carry all these bags of trauma alone. She gave me the tools to lighten the load, but I had to be willing and keep an open mind. I had to hear her out. Eventually, I was going twice a month and then once a week. To be completely honest, there was never a time in those three years when I questioned if the investment was worth it. Investing in your self-care will always be worth it.

In Chapter 3, I mentioned that, when I told some of the closest people in my life that I was thinking about going to therapy, I was met with questioning and shame. Hell, all I said was that I was *thinking* about it, and you would have thought I'd told them I was quitting my job and going to backpack through Europe. One of my relatives even dared to say that I didn't need those people; I could talk to them because they knew me better than I knew myself. At that moment, I was hurt, mad, and speechless. I vowed never to talk to them about it ever again. And to this day, I haven't talked about my experience in therapy with that person, but I still love them. I have learned that my healing is not dictated by what others think. Healing is for me.

I want to take a moment to dig deeper into this idea that we, as women of color, sometimes feel we need to seek approval from others. Systemic racism was created to make us feel like we aren't ever good enough. Because all our life we've had to fight, the validation of others can be a safe place. But it's a place I hope we evacuate sooner rather than later. We can't live our lives by other people's rules. It has never served us in history. When Shirley Chisholm ran for president in 1972, even the women in the women's movement tried to get her to step aside. Those women were her friends and were supposed to be fighting for all women at that time, but the fight looks different when us Black women decide we want a seat at the table too. Chisholm didn't play by anyone else's rules, and she sure as heck didn't ask or wait for permission to pursue her dreams. Therefore, she was unbought and unbossed. We need to channel some of her energy. We can be unbought and unbossed, too, on our journey to healing.

Dr. Joy Harden Bradford of *Therapy for Black Girls* made an important point about not feeling like we have to seek validation or acceptance from the people we love if we decide to see a therapist. She said, "Be cautious with who you share your healing journey with. Some people will only seek to get us off our path to healing." She also dropped this gem: "You don't have to tell everyone; let them see firsthand how you're healing once you've gone—they will see something different about you." Man, oh man, do I wish I had that advice back then, but I am so glad I get to pass it along to you.

I also spoke to Ashley McGirt, a licensed mental health therapist who owns and operates Ashley McGirt Counseling Services and specializes in racial trauma. I wanted to dissect the role our families play in choosing therapy and discussions around mental health. McGirt said, "In Black families, language has to matter." She went on to tell me a story about one of her relatives who was suffering from a mental illness. At the time, no one knew what the real situation was regarding this relative. She recalls always hearing the family joke about so-and-so taking their meds. Whenever this person came around, folks would still poke fun. Later in life, they found out she was bipolar, yet that offensive language and joking persisted. I am sure McGirt's family members aren't the only ones who do this; I am sure we have all made these jokes or been around someone who has. McGirt mentioned that the language many of our families use is due to "limited exposure and projecting." Yet this is an "opportunity to create boundaries, and part of healing is setting your boundaries."

It's essential to surround yourself with supportive people and set boundaries on your healing, because, as McGirt said, "the world is already trying to take our breath away."

HEALING IS A CHOICE

If you get nothing else from this book, the one thing I pray you take away is that healing is your choice. Meaning, no one else should get to dictate what tools you use to heal. No one else on earth should feel they have the agency to decide how healing should look for you. In the back of my head, I should have known not to bring my decision up to certain people. I knew deep down they might not be ready to embrace alternative routes to mental wellness. But, then again, alternative to what? Who gets to decide what is mainstream healing? I know they probably felt like they were being supportive, but that kind of support almost stopped me from getting what I needed to manage my trauma. Please guard your choice. It's the one misstep I made before going to therapy, and those family members' critical words rattled in my head longer than they should have. The moral of the story is you don't have to tell everyone what you're doing. In an ideal world, we would love to share important decisions like these with our family and friends. Sometimes, the people closest to you can be the ones who unintentionally sow seeds of doubt, when they should be considering some therapy themselves. Like Solange said, "When you even feeling it from your own." Somebody send Solange an offering, because that will preach. Sometimes it be your own! But please don't let them stop you.

With that said, I won't lie to you and tell you I didn't feel shame at first. For probably the first ten sessions, I was like, *What are you doing, Minda?* Or I would be sitting in the lobby waiting for my session, and I would tell myself, *I am not like them. They probably are here for some heavy sh*t.* And here we go again. How in the hell am I going to sit in the same lobby for the same service and try to throw shade? That is why my butt ended up being there once a week. When I left California, I was doing virtual sessions. I swear we can be our own worst nightmare at times. The stories we tell ourselves, positive or negative, can be the most harmful. As women of color, we deal with a lot just walking out our door in the morning. There's so much trauma that comes with just being us that we cannot afford to inflict more pain upon ourselves.

I had a conversation with Farah Harris, licensed clinical professional therapist and founder of WorkingWell Daily. Harris works with Black women to identify how to maintain their mental and emotional well-being in racially charged work environments. I asked her what she thought were some of the obstacles that tend to get in the way of women of color and our healing. She made three profound points:

1. We have to dismantle this glorified myth that if you are a strong woman, you can't ask for help. A strong woman is wise enough to ask for help when she needs it.
2. People think that if we center our needs as women, we are being selfish. But seeking healing is a form of selflessness.

3. It's okay to feel what you're feeling. You might feel angry, isolated, and in pain, but we don't have to stay in it. It's okay to honor your feelings and your voice.

THE CONSEQUENCES

I remember being a couple of months into my therapy sessions with Rashid, and I had a friend visiting from out of town. We were coming back from a brunch spot in Los Angeles called Jack n' Jill's Too. We were about a block away from my house, and walking toward us was Rashid. I didn't know if I should say hi, pretend I didn't know her, or introduce her. Mostly, I wanted to grab my friend and turn around because I still felt some shame and didn't want to have to talk about who this lady was. At any rate, Rashid and I walked past each other, nodded, and smiled. My friend said, "Do you know that lady?" I nervously laughed and said, "Kinda," and returned to our conversation. The rest of the day, I was in my head, wondering if Rashid thought I might be acting shady because I barely spoke. *Ugh, clearly this will be a thing I will need to unpack when I see her next Thursday.* I was really just caught off guard seeing her on a Saturday afternoon.

But my real come-to-Jesus moment that ultimately helped me move past my shame was this: What would be the consequence if I didn't allow myself to heal from all the traumas I was experiencing, and not just the racialized ones? I realized that being whole outweighed anything else. I hope you won't allow shame to stop you from your healing either. I'd rather put in the work and heal than sit in my pain and never know what freedom feels like. I would rather see Rashid weekly and know the person I could be with my mind and body healed, versus never meeting the healed version of myself. Shame detours our healing and helps us stay stuck in our suffering, but we can choose to shut shame down. Shame doesn't have to control our narrative.

I think it's important to highlight the consequence of not allowing ourselves to heal. Because I believe there is one, whether you want to admit it or not. But don't take my word for it—let's see what the experts have to say. I asked Farah Harris and Ashley McGirt what the consequence could potentially be if women of color don't permit themselves to heal, and their answers blew me away. Harris said, "Yes, we rob ourselves and the people who love us from experiencing who we really are." McGirt made the point even more strongly: "The consequence is death."

The National Institutes of Health (NIH) says, "Black women have higher rates of undetected diseases, illness, chronic conditions, and shorter life expectancy than other groups." The NIH suggests that Black women are "particularly vulnerable to the impacts of race-related stress and this can cause arteries to narrow, making it harder to lose weight—especially dangerous belly fat—and raise blood pressure and risk for heart attack." You see, McGirt wasn't being morbid when she said "death." If we don't learn to manage our stress, then it could lead to that.

But McGirt also offered some sage advice: "Allow yourself to mourn, allow yourself to heal, and find ways to limit your exposure to racially related stress by exercising and eating healthier diets." Thinking about what she said makes me wonder how many of our ancestors died due to workplace racial stress. According to the Anxiety and Depression Association of America, Black women, in particular, suffer from higher rates of anxiety disorders than our white counterparts. But that makes a lot of sense when we have to be the strong Black woman while trying not to be the angry Black woman—of course we are stressed as hell. Harris and McGirt's advice shook me because I am so much better to myself and the people who love me when I am not wounded. We have the opportunity to break the curse.

THE HIGHS AND LOWS

I have to tell you that—even though I had wanted to pretend that Rashid was somebody I used to know—eventually I got comfortable with her as we established a relationship. And I would end up seeing Rashid walking on the street often, because she lived in the neighborhood. Building trust with your therapist is vital. It took me a while to let my guard down. Not because she wasn't doing her job, but because I wasn't ready to do the heavy lifting right away. That is why it's crucial to make sure you want to enter into a relationship with this person, because at times you will feel like you are in a Drake video, runnin' through the 6 with your woes and on top of the world. In other sessions, you will feel worse than when you walked through the door. Sometimes my emotions were all over the damn place. I wasn't prepared to be talking about my racist colleague and then, in the next few minutes, discuss some connection back to that time in third grade I had suppressed. Next thing you know, it's no longer about the racist colleague—it's my childhood. There were sessions I wanted to go deeper, and there were sessions I just wanted her to shut the hell up and stop asking me so many questions. I had never considered myself an angry person, but God knows there were days when I marched back to my apartment.

I only tell you this because some of these visits won't feel like Disneyland. I had no idea the real work that I would be embarking on as I sat on Rashid's couch for the first time. Doing the work isn't just some cute thing to say; it's a commitment to yourself and your mental health. I am not telling you this to scare you away. I want you to understand why Molly has an attitude sometimes in her therapy sessions on *Insecure*—that stuff is real.

I remember one session in particular when Rashid had me digging too deep. We were investigating why I was always being called a "rising star" and how my title and pay didn't reflect any rising. I was beyond fed up, and I thought we would have a session on why my managers sucked. Instead, we dug into why I hadn't advocated for myself. I was so annoyed, and I canceled three sessions because I needed a minute to catch my breath. And then, in another session, we had a significant breakthrough moment, and I brought her a gift the next session. I was a mess, but a beautiful mess. With that said, I don't think I would be where I am today without leaning into my courage. It takes courage to want more for yourself. It takes courage to stand up to yourself and others and fight like hell for your mental state. And it takes a lot of courage to say that you won't let this world of racial oppression stop you from being who the creator intended you to be.

There were moments when I wasn't sure I could push through, but I never had to struggle alone. Rashid was like the midwife helping me push out all the years of corporate trauma that almost tried to take me out. I can honestly say that I would have never been able to write my first book, *The Memo*, had I not allowed myself to address my workplace pain. Maya Angelou said, "You may not control all the events that happen to you, but you can decide not to be reduced by them." I might still be hurting had I never gone down this road.

A COMMITMENT

Therapy will require a few things from you. First, you must have the ability to be honest with yourself. Second, healing isn't a sprint; it's a marathon. Don't think it will take one or two sessions to undo years of workplace trauma or any other trauma. Third, if you don't find the right therapist on the first try, please make a promise that you won't throw in the towel. Promise yourself you will fight for the right tools and the right healer. Therapists are healers used by God, in my opinion. I believe God has given many people on this earth gifts to help others, such as doctors, lawyers, and teachers. Would we not consider them healers too? Let's learn to expand who has the ability to help us reach wellness. Additionally, there are some things that your therapist won't be to you. Let me tell you something that you must know from the jump: your therapist is not your best friend. Please don't confuse what your relationship is and what it isn't. No matter how many laughs y'all share, no matter how real they keep it with you, they are there to provide you a service. I just don't want you to get your feelings hurt. As much as Rashid knows about me, we have never gone out to dinner and we don't discuss what happened on *The Real Housewives of Potomac.* I have never confused my relationship with her. Although, I think in a different situation we might have been friends.

I AIN'T GOT IT

I realize that just because I told you that your company or organization might have an EAP and shared my experience the first time I went to therapy, that might not be enough evidence to convince you that therapy is a tool that could work for you. Or perhaps you're interested, but therapy isn't a financial option for you right now. Or perhaps the therapists you've met with don't have much training or experience in helping clients work through racial trauma. When I spoke to our experts, I tried to anticipate some of your needs so that I could share with you advice that could help you work toward healing today, even if therapy doesn't seem accessible to you at the moment.

As one example of an area where you might need help, please consider how many years you've been code-switching at work. You know the times when you walk into your job and you see your white colleague Bob and in your most proper voice, you say, "Hello, Bob, it's been quite some time since I've seen you. How are Margie and the kids?" As you continue down the hallway, you run into your fellow colleague of color Patrice, and you greet her entirely differently. Patrice walks toward you and she says, "Hey, girl, hey—I was trying to call you this weekend, where were you?" and you laugh and say, "Girl, I was where the money resides." Then you both kiki like it's *Def Comedy Jam*. You would probably never use that phrase around Bob or other white people in the office. Yet you consider Patrice someone you can let your hair down with and you don't have to be so buttoned-up. That is just one example of code-switching that we tend to do. Another example of code-switching was in 2012, when our former president, Barack Obama, was meeting the US men's Olympic basketball team. When President Obama greeted one of the white coaches, he gave him a hearty and healthy handshake. When he greeted basketball player Kevin Durant, they pretty much dapped and gave each other a hug.

Many of us probably don't even realize we are code-switching because we've been doing it all our lives. But have you ever sat back and thought about how draining that is? I am not saying don't be "professional" in the workplace. But much of our authentic selves, white people never end up seeing. We walk around on eggshells most of the day because we don't want to come across as "too much of . . . "—and you can fill in the blank. When I spoke with Farah Harris, she mentioned the psychological consequences that code-switching and microaggressions can take on us. She said, "What is disappointing as a clinician is that I see how my Black clients find ways to successfully navigate the workplace and white spaces by using high emotional intelligence professionally but fail to use it in their personal lives. Ideally, I would love to see more Black people adjust their EQ [emotional quotient, or the ability to recognize emotions in yourself and others] as a self-care tool where they can create healthy mental and emotional boundaries, assertively use their voice, and acknowledge and process their feelings, particularly when experiencing race-based trauma." Harris isn't suggesting that we can change the way our colleagues act toward us. But we can establish healthy boundaries, which she is encouraging us to learn how to set. Essentially, Harris is telling us that it's okay to choose ourselves, and that is one of the many steps toward healing.

The ugly truth of being a woman of color in the workplace is that most of us entered into our positions knowing that we might encounter racism. It saddens me that racism is inevitable in most white-majority workspaces. The problem is, no one ever told us how taxing that racism would become. No one ever warned us that eventually that harm becomes pretty painful. And no one ever talked about how we heal from it and how we can become right within. I mean, how do we continue to work when at any given time there might be another Black Lives Matter march right outside our window? No one ever talks about that part. Racial trauma is nothing we should take lightly. I am here to tell you that healing is available to us—hell, healing is necessary for us—so that we can be our best selves. Maybe it won't be via therapy for you. But I guarantee you will need some tools so that we don't lose the best parts of you that were chipped away by racial trauma.

Ashley McGirt encourages women of color to "take a break." She believes that many of the racial aggressions that we experience in the workplace are constant, and many of us have told ourselves that we have to push through it. But she is offering another road to healing, and it includes resting when we might need to remove ourselves from those toxic situations. So when the next microaggression comes your way, you might not be in a position to quit—nor am I suggesting that—but you might be able to take a fifteen-minute break. Or maybe you need to take some vacation days a little sooner than you planned. Or, on those days when you are not sure what to do or who to call, McGirt recommends Therapist Aid (www.therapistaid.com), a website with free and affordable interactive therapy tools. The site provides a host of resources that can aid in your healing journey. It might even be something you try before you reach out to a therapist. With that said, I am not endorsing this service or resource—yet I wanted to make you aware of it. In the end, I just want to make sure you have resources to get through the day whenever Bob says something that he can't take back and doesn't want to take responsibility for how it made you feel. We can't control Bob's healing journey, but we can be very intentional about ours.

STIGMA

I don't believe therapy has as much of a stigma as it used to when I was growing up, and that is a blessing. According to a *Washington Post* article from 2013 titled "Therapists Say African Americans Are Increasingly Seeking Help for Mental Illness," some practitioners had seen an increase of African Americans going to therapy over the previous ten years of up to 25 percent. I imagine that number has only increased since, especially during 2020, which was one of the most racially charged moments in my lifetime.

I am forever grateful for my therapist. She helped me navigate through a lot of my trauma. There were days I left her office light as a feather, and there were days I felt the pain of suppressed emotions that made me want to run to my bed and put my phone on silent. It takes work, y'all—I can't express that enough. But the other thing to remember is that some of us have worked with career coaches on various parts of our career journey, so why not view a therapist in the same way? Therapy is coaching for your emotional and mental health. And don't forget that healing takes courage. Brené Brown said it best: "Courage starts with showing up and letting ourselves be seen." If we are suffering from trauma, it's hard to let ourselves be seen, because, let's be honest, we don't even want to see ourselves. Healing isn't easy, but I believe it's worth it. At the end of my conversation with Ashley McGirt, she said, "Healing looks like work." What type of work are you willing to do to achieve your healing? The cool thing is, you get to decide what that answer is based on what makes sense for where you are right now in your life.

I wish I could call you or send you a message and see what's swirling around your head right now. I know this information might sound heavy. Hopefully you are curious enough to see if therapy might be an option for you. There are even faith-based therapists if you want a mixture of both approaches. I hope that the more we talk out loud about treatment, the more the myth that only certain people have access to healing will vanish. I don't know your work experiences or what you might currently be dealing with, but one thing I know for sure is I am confident you can find the tools that are right for you. Because just like Oprah once said on *Super Soul Sunday*, "We are to learn from one another's pain." I hope this chapter helped you learn that you don't have to stay wounded, be-cause if we don't heal, we could potentially hurt others too. I am rooting for you!

Time to Unpack and Reassess

1. What feelings or emotions are coming up for you right now?
2. Is therapy a tool you might consider using? Why or why not?
3. If you are considering therapy, what are your concerns? What are your goals?
4. Write a letter to yourself from the future, describing how therapy has helped you heal, and how you are thriving and experiencing freedom for the first time thanks to the work you did.
5. What boundaries will you need to set if you choose to use therapy as a tool in your healing tool kit?
6. If you've used therapy in the past, what do you think you will need this time around that you didn't get from your last therapist?

Chapter 5

HOW WILL I KNOW

How will I know
Hey, how will I know
—Whitney Houston,
"How Will I Know"

Healing is an interesting concept. I've always heard healing talked about in biblical terms. Growing up in church you tend to learn about healing through the lens of the denomination you were exposed to. As I've gotten older, I've been able to redefine healing in my own terms. I thought that healing only occurred when someone had to overcome a life-threatening physical ailment or when they've experienced a loss. The preacher would encourage the congregation to come to the altar and receive their healing immediately, as if it could only happen on Sunday mornings. And yes, healing is necessary for those situations. Yet I think the part that some preachers don't convey in that altar call is that sometimes healing doesn't happen in an instant. You can't always put your trauma on a microwavable plate, pop it in, hit the thirty-second button, and, boom, *Come get it girl! Your healing is ready.* I wish healing was that simple. Yet for some of us, we might be pursuing our healing each and every day until we take our last breath on this planet.

NO TIMETABLE

Healing cannot be on a timeline. It is definitely not on your or my planned timetable; I think it has a mind of its own. What I do believe, though, is that healing is about using the right tools so that you can continue to thrive and not just survive in the workplace. I think healing in many ways is tied to faith. In Hebrews 11:1, faith is referenced in this way: "Now faith is the substance of things hoped for, the evidence of things not seen." I feel like healing might work similarly on occasion. Just because we don't physically see healing happening doesn't mean we aren't benefiting from it being in motion. The real question is, do we have enough faith to believe that we deserve equality over acceptance? Do we have enough faith that the next time one of our colleagues racially assaults us, we won't put our heads down or look the other way? Do we have enough faith to keep our heads held high and look them in the eye? All it takes is a small seed of faith to let healing be our guide and help us continue toward growth.

Personally, I consider the process of healing from my racialized trauma to be a lifelong practice. Especially if you are a person of color in the United States, I don't know that we will ever truly heal from the past and ongoing sins of this country. With that said, I still believe we have the ability to reconcile our pain and find freedom on our terms.

We do not have to wait for Congress to pass legislation to force people to see us as equals before we can find some inner peace. Now don't get me wrong. We need those laws, because some people don't know how to do right on their own. But healing has allowed me to redefine the norms. I am no longer waiting for white people to finally wake up one day and say, *I guess Black lives do matter.* I started to realize that healing for me had to happen first in my mind.

A MINDSET SHIFT

So much of our existence in corporate, nonprofit, and academic spaces has been a lived experience of code-switching. W. E. B. Du Bois uses the term "double-consciousness," which I prefer over "code-switching." It's this notion that the dominant majority created norms that benefit and center themselves, and we (people of color) have had to play double Dutch trying to follow their rules and keep some of our authenticity along the way. We have always felt like our identity has been forfeited to assimilate into white culture. Du Bois put it frankly: "Looking at one's self through the eyes of someone else." He brought about this framework in 1903 and many of us are still dealing with the effects of living double lives in the workplace. So much for bringing your authentic self to work. But I think "Can I be authentic at work?" is the wrong question. Instead, we need to discuss *whose* version of authenticity we are talking about.

Many of us aren't simply trying to find healing because some white person butchered our name once or twice. We aren't necessarily exploring what healing could look like because someone called us the N-word a time or two. It's the constant and compounded racial trauma that we are born into this world with. This is also intergenerational trauma. Many of us are still feeling the trauma of our ancestors from four-hundred-plus years ago. Dr. Martin Luther King Jr. said that racism "scars the soul and distorts the personality." When you feel racial oppression at work, in your car, at a restaurant, or at the park, it can be hard to reconcile being Black in this country, because so many of our experiences are as second-class citizens. I might not see "colored" and "white" signs anymore, but every time I sit in first class, I feel the stares. I feel people questioning whether I am in the right seat, or asking themselves how I got here. I feel that not only from other passengers but sometimes from the flight staff. So hell yeah racism distorts the personality; it's hard for it not to. That is why healing is crucial. We don't want to lose who we are and who we are destined to become. My healing started to take place when I found that I was able to possess long-lasting peace, rather than continue living in a constant state of anxiety at work. Rather than wake up with dread about the next microaggression, I started to empower myself by putting strategies in place to protect myself and make my work life better each day. When I began to use the resources available to me in my career, I started incorporating daily practices of peace and implementing actions that help the racialized trauma dissipate over time. But that had to start in my mind. And I had to learn to be right within. I had to unlearn old lies and narratives that had held me back.

GET YOU SOME PEACE

When we allow the pain to move out of our lives, we can finally live in peace. Unfortunately, sometimes the pain can be comfortable for us because it's all we've known. In this chapter, we will discuss how to detect if healing is taking root in your life. It may be strange to be talking about measuring your healing in the middle of a book about healing. You might be thinking, *Hey, let's go through the steps of this book and then evaluate our success at the end.* But as I've said before, healing is a process. There is no natural stopping point; you are always going to be learning and growing, and the challenges ahead will always be changing. Also, seeing your progress at healing can motivate you to continue this important work.

Now, I would be doing both of us a disservice by not acknowledging that it might be hard to determine if steps toward healing are manifesting in your life. In this book I share with you the tools that helped me process my racial trauma. Sometimes we just need to know it's possible. My advice is by no means meant to stop you from using additional resources on your healing journey. My belief is you can never have too many tools. You pick up the ones you need when you need them. The worst thing is to feel like you are being racially assaulted and not have the resources you need to help you pull through. And I know the phrase "pull through" can seem dramatic, but our emotional and physical well-being is critical to a healthy and long life. Healing is definitely a journey, and I hope to provide you some guideposts along the way so you can continue moving forward. For those moments when you might want to retreat into the comfort of trauma, I will be here coaching you back to the place you last shook hands with healing herself. I will provide you with some key steps as you lean into your faith, push aside your skepticism, and take action to experience peace, joy, and happiness, even when things get tough.

In Japanese culture, *kintsugi* is an artistic way of putting broken pottery pieces back together with gold. The reassembled pottery is often considered more beautiful than the piece in its original state. It is said that *kintsugi* takes work and a certain awareness, much like it takes to bring about healing. At times in my career, I have felt like broken pottery pieces. I have felt like corporate America tossed me to and fro, not handling me with care. It has taken a lot of work to put myself back together into a new and beautiful masterpiece. There is healing after feeling broken. I remember when I left one workplace in the fall of 2014. I left that toxic environment feeling like pieces of myself were scattered all over the office, and I'd have to use a small broom to sweep them up. But by that stage it was hard to recognize those pieces as having once been parts of myself. I was so racially traumatized that I became confused about who I was, what my career potential could be, and how to value myself. But even in my most painful moments, I took some of those pieces back, because I had faith that, at some point, some of them would produce a beautiful surprise. Those pieces that I swept up that day, I turned them into gold. I decided to turn my trauma into triumph.

ARE WE THERE YET?

Before we move on, I want to share a little more with you about the importance of our mental wellness. Throughout this book, we will discuss how mental hygiene is something that should be a priority in our lives. Even when you think that you are strong enough to make it through anything, there will be situations that might pop up that you weren't expecting.

For example, for most of the time while I was writing this book, I was sitting in the middle of a global pandemic, working from home for months. As Charles Dickens said, "It was the best of times, it was the worst of times." And I couldn't help but think about all the Black women and women of color—hell, just people of color in general—who at one point had to deal with racial assaults while they were in a work environment. On days like that, the only thing that used to get most of us through it was knowing that at the end of the workday we could go home, to the bar, or to someone's house and have a moment of venting and peace. But in the pandemic, many of us haven't had that safe space to run to anymore. Now, people of color are being racially assaulted in their home, a place that used to be a refuge, through their computer screen. They are sitting on their couch or in their favorite chair while someone says some sh*t they shouldn't. Right outside the door (if they are lucky enough to have a closed home-office space) or down the hall are their kids, roommate, or partner. Imagine dealing with everyday racism and never being able to leave your house. And while that's going on, we see one senseless Black shooting after another. It's a hard pill to swallow. And it's a lot of trauma to unpack.

When racialized situations like that hit the fan, it's hard to know if you are healing or not. It's hard to stay mentally fit. I mean, I currently work for myself and I still have been racially insulted and underpaid for my services during quarantine. I am reconciling being an advocate working to dismantle oppressive systems in the workplace for women of color and knowing that I am in the most racialized time period of my life thus far. At one point, I had pulled into a Target parking lot to stock up on some snacks and face wash. The police shooting of Jacob Blake had just transpired in Kenosha, Wisconsin. I was about to get out of my car, and I saw a white man and child laughing and smiling. I busted out in tears. I knew at that moment, there was only one America: one where white people are thriving and Black people per usual are trying to figure out how to survive. I cried a deep, heavy cry, and I couldn't stop. What broke me out of my crying spell was my blue mask sitting on the passenger's seat. I thought, *Well, with these glasses and my mask no one will know I've been crying.* And yes, this is America: the home of the brave and what I've been told is the land of the free. Yet many of us are questioning how long freedom will really last.

It was that moment in the parking lot when I knew that I had to allow myself to feel my feelings, but also that I couldn't let myself stay there for too long. I have worked too hard to relapse. I couldn't afford to. There are too many people counting on me, and if I succumb to the oppression, then I can't fight one of the biggest battles of our lives. And with the biggest battle, I need to be like David: ready to slay Goliath.

In this case, racism is the Goliath in this country. None of us can fight a good battle if we don't have a determined mindset. Meaning I will do whatever it takes to keep my healing moving forward. My life depends on it.

IT'S TIME FOR THE PERCOLATOR

Oh, and not only does my life depend on it, but yours does too. So now you might be thinking, *How will I know if or when healing is percolating?* I want to walk you through a framework that continues to help me understand and process my healing journey. Public and motivational speaker Les Brown said, "You can't see the picture when you're in the frame." And that rings true with healing. Sometimes when we are too close to our situation, we might not feel that any change has occurred. It might be a day or a year or even decades later when you see that your road down healing boulevard was actually worth the trip. In the next chapter, we will discuss maintenance strategies to help you through your process and reconciliation. There, you will also find some affirmations to help you continue to stay mentally fit day-to-day. At the end of the book, I will provide you with some resources to help prevent possible racial relapses, because healing is a daily practice.

I created what I call the Racial Mosaic Framework (RMF). I chose the word "mosaic" because the dictionary defines it as "the process of making a surface decoration made by inlaying small pieces of variously colored material to form pictures or patterns." I am a firm believer that words matter. I want you to know that you can assemble a picture of healing, but first you might need to know what that picture could look like. In the RMF, there are five actions to help you monitor how your healing is progressing or regressing: Acknowledgment, Decision-Making, Accountability, Drawing Your Line, and Vibrating Higher. I know these actions might sound a bit strange, but if you have come this far in the book, you might as well continue reading and hear me out.

As we move through the five steps, you might see how you can use this advice whenever you are met with a microaggression or a situation that feels racialized. Think about how you could use these steps to detach yourself from the racialized event and recenter yourself. Let's dive in!

Acknowledgment

Before I started my healing journey, I was the type of person who was always in my head. If someone said something to me that I felt in my stomach was racialized, I would dwell on it the entire workday. I would then let the situation fester in my mind when I got home from work. The part I hated the most was that sometimes these racialized experiences would keep me up at night, because I was still thinking about them. The crappy thing about racialized situations in the workplace is that you can be enjoying your day at work, returning to your desk after an amazing chicken-salad sandwich, just the way you like it. Then, the next thing you know, you feel like you are in the 1960s *Batman* TV series and—*Boom! Pow! Ka-Pow!*—you've been punched with racial aggression out of nowhere by some white lady named Jill. I guess Jill wasn't there on unconscious-bias training day.

The reality is that some people will never get themselves together and be a good human. We can't leave our healing in someone else's hands, because if you are waiting for someone like Jill to center you, it might never happen. I was able to continue my healing journey by using various tools as part of my personalized treatment plan, but then I was met with situations with colleagues or managers like Jill. Thankfully, I was able to manage those situations in my mind and with my emotions so I wouldn't go cuckoo for Cocoa Puffs every day at work. When racialized situations happened before, I didn't always have the language to articulate how I felt or know if it was even okay to feel upset, disappointed, and disrespected. For the majority of my career, I have been told, "It is what it is" and "Just keep your head down." Now I am in the process of unlearning so many of these well-intentioned narratives that were passed down to me, which seemed to offer ways to survive as a Black woman in the workplace. I hate to say it, but all advice ain't good advice.

One of the most frequently asked questions I encounter after a speaking engagement is: How do you know when it's time to move on from your current work environment after you've experienced so many racial insults and assaults? It's a question I've had to answer for myself, and I offer my audiences the same answer. The bottom line is, we know when we are being mistreated. We feel it in every part of our bones. We can't spin our wheels trying to figure out if every bad experience at work was racial or not. We can't spend our energy trying to figure out all the reasons someone might respond to another human in ways that try to strip them of their dignity. But what I know to be true is, if it bothers you, that's all that matters, full stop. Regardless of someone's intent, it made you feel crappy. You have a choice. You can stay, you can go, or you can start to plan your exit strategy. Only you know what your personal situation allows you to do. But we both know when someone is wrong.

I used an example of how acknowledging a racialized experience in real time can help you heal, yet this framework is also designed to assess how you feel about past racialized trauma. Can you name what caused you harm in your past that still triggers you today? Maybe there is a time that has been too painful to even allow yourself to think about. How will you know if your healing is taking root? You will finally be able to acknowledge it. Acknowledging it is critical, and if you are able to say what it is, even if only to yourself, that is a huge feat. Please don't discount how naming racialized experiences as such can help you take some power back from your past.

Now the issue we are up against is that it takes a lot of energy to recover after being on the receiving end of someone's "good intentions." But don't for one minute think you aren't good enough to deserve the peace and freedom that many of our ancestors never got to experience. For so long, we have been conditioned to not even be able to call a thing a thing. And the thing I am referring to is racism. In my former career, every racialized experience I had, I felt like I could never call it racism out loud. I was scared. I feared what saying the truth might lead to. It was clear that everyone else was comfortable living with the lies. Even on those days when I knew it was racism, I tried to convince myself it couldn't be. So, allow yourself to acknowledge and name racism, because that is where your freedom lies, in telling the truth. This country has been comfortable far too long with the lies of racism. Trust me, you will feel so much better leaning into what you know is true and centering yourself.

What are those past racialized occurrences that you might need to name in order to be able to move forward? And why haven't you allowed yourself to name them? I am sure there are a lot of reasons, but if you haven't been able to write the experience down, say it out loud, or tell someone you trust, that might indicate that you've stalled in the process of healing. Either way, I believe it's important to be able to track our healing progress, and if you are there, awesome, and if you still have some healing to do, that is okay too. We are not in a race to the healing finish line. Just be aware of where you are on your journey, and I hope that one day you will be able to name it.

Decision-Making

Once we are able to name the ugliness that has happened to us, then we are able to move on and articulate our truth. The truth can only be defined by you. This is where you decide if you want to address the situation that has occurred or if your mental health is calling for you to leave it where it is. This step can help you go back and work through some past racialized occurrences. It can even prepare you for unexpected microaggressions in the future. In deciding how you want to handle the situation and articulate your truth, you might decide to document past occurrences, so that if the situation ever called for it, you would have all your receipts ready. You may never go to HR with the racialized occurrence, but if you ever needed to, you'd have your ducks in a row. Or if you wanted to contact the Equal Employment Opportunity Commission (EEOC), you would have evidence for your case. Or you might decide you need to lay things out plain and clear with your colleague, to say that you will not tolerate being discriminated against and if it happens again you will report it.

The other part of your decision-making process is deciding not to blame yourself for the racialized offense. Because most of us have spent our entire lives in a racist country and workplace, we often will blame ourselves and try to imagine how we could have de-escalated the situation. In the end, the situation had nothing to do with you making the wrong move and everything to do with the person who racially assaulted you. The bottom line is, once you are able to document the occurrences, my hope is that you will know that you're healing because you can finally formally articulate your truth. I know that is not an easy thing to do. It took years before I was able to speak about many of my racialized workplace moments.

Accountability

We have to place blame on the perpetrator. Let's say you have been planning a big family reunion for two years. On the day of the meetup, it starts to rain cats and dogs at the park you reserved. None of your family members would be mad at you because it started to rain out of nowhere. And if they did blame you for the rain, that would be pretty absurd, right? The same is true when someone at work discriminates against you. Never blame yourself for what transpired. If you are still holding onto guilt due to the hurt that someone has caused you, I hope you will learn to release yourself from it.

You can't control what's inside someone's heart, especially when it harbors hatred due to the color of their colleagues' skin. It's about time we hold accountable those who caused the harm. It's up to us to be the keepers of the truth. As women of color, we have a legacy of trauma, and somebody has to take responsibility and it can't be us. You will know that you are in the process of healing when you no longer blame yourself for the racialized experiences from the past or those that might happen in the future.

I remember early in my career feeling like I was walking on eggshells when a racialized situation took place. If I tried to address it, I would be met with opposition, and then the conversation would end with me saying something like, "Oh I must have misunderstood what you meant. I apologize." For the love of God, so many times we have apologized for their sins. We have apologized when we haven't even done anything wrong, yet we are met with having to make everything right and take the higher road. I am tired of it and you should be too.

In 2020, Angela Davis was asked in multiple interviews about racism and police reform in this country, and she said, "We must stop assuming that one person is responsible for harm." The same is true at work about your colleagues who might racially assault you—they are not working alone. Managers have enabled them; colleagues have turned a blind eye. Racism doesn't work alone; it has a crew. If we continue to blame ourselves, we can't hold the perpetrators accountable and we end up taking on more BS to carry in our bags. Remember, we are trying to pack light here, because if we don't we will be compromising our healing. And it's hard to be right within when we are carrying those racialized bags.

Drawing Your Line

The next point I want to make might be one of the toughest to manage. But you said you wanted to know if you are healing or not, right? Once you've started to experience healing and begin to utilize your healing tools, learn to move forward. Don't let it fester. When you get to the point on your healing journey when you can draw your line and see people for who they are, you won't allow anyone to harm you again. How many times does the ghost of Maya Angelou have to tell you? "When someone shows you who they are, believe them the first time."

Now let me be clear. I am not saying you are allowing people to mistreat you at work. What I am saying is, you have put boundaries in place so that their vile words or actions don't cause secondary infections like they used to. You are finally able to see the enemy for who they are, and now you can take steps to protect yourself from their venom. Before healing took root, we would be shocked and surprised. *Like OMG, I can't believe Brenda said that to me!* Come on girl, your white colleague Brenda might have seemed like a work friend, but she has been saying crap like that since you started working there. Drawing your line is by no means giving anyone a pass, but you know you can't get down with Brenda like that anymore! And you can't allow her in your space like you used to.

What I mean by moving forward: once you have gone through some of the other steps, you understand and can spot patterns that you've seen before with others who might have racially aggressed you. After the first couple times, you don't have to wait for them to microaggress you five more times before you call it what it is: a pattern of abuse. You'll learn to respond earlier, to set your boundaries earlier, because you understand how critical drawing your line is for your continued healing. This step also helps keep us accountable. We won't continue to tell ourselves, *They don't mean any harm.* You can't know their intentions, and, honestly, even if they didn't intend the harm, it is their responsibility to acknowledge the harm as real, and it is their responsibility to make it right.

This entire framework is meant to center your right to have your pain acknowledged and taken seriously. As we continue to heal, we can't make excuses for the harm experienced by communities of color for generations. There comes a time when we must draw our line and establish boundaries. We will know that we are healing when we are establishing boundaries that set our continued healing up for success. I will address what setting boundaries in relation to this framework looks like later in this chapter.

Before I move to the last pillar, I have to tell you a story of how I knew I was healing and growing. I had to draw my line in the sand with a colleague who I thought was a friend.

In one of my earlier jobs, I would travel from city to city and stay on-site with a client for three months to a year. The length of the contract depended on the needs of the client.

My next assignment would be in the South. I had never been to this state before, and at the time I thought, *Oh no, do they like Black people in this state?* I guess you could say I had my own biases. I heard that the city I was traveling to was pretty liberal and had a great nightlife, and that I shouldn't have any problems. But, to be fair, all of this was coming from my white colleagues. I was the only Black woman consultant at that firm. To make a long story short, I found out that a colleague would also be assigned to the project. He was a white man I'll call Danny, and I had gotten along with him well by that point. Or so I had thought.

I found out about my new assignment two weeks before I was to arrive, and I had no housing set up. The apartment that my mom helped secure for me wouldn't be ready until a month after I arrived. I assumed I would just have the firm pay for my hotel and that would be that. Well, Danny told me he had just scored a large house outside the town we were assigned to. He invited me to stay in the spare room. At first I was like *Nah*, but he insisted. I thought about it. I would be working long hours, so I guessed the only thing I would really need was a clean place to sleep and shower. I kept telling myself that it was a short time and it might be fun. I also thought I might get lonely, and since I had never been to the area before, it might be safer for me as a woman. At least that was the story I told myself.

When we started working together, everything was going fine. But there was one thing I didn't realize was taking place. I was thriving in this new environment and Danny started to get jealous of me. Well, at least I initially thought it was jealousy. But later I realized it was resentment fueled by racism and sexism. I also have to tell you that Danny and I were told that one of us would be promoted after this contract. Looking back, that was such a horrible thing for our manager to tell us. I guess it really is a dog-eat-dog world. The one who got promoted would then oversee our own staff and take over another contract. I didn't think I would have any problems because I thought Danny was a friend and we weren't in competition with each other. I thought, *I would love the opportunity, but I would be equally happy for him.* I thought we were like family. I mean, damn, I was staying at his home and eating dinner with him. What ended up happening next was like a sucker punch. Even when you're healing, sucker punches may happen, but it's how you handle them that counts.

A couple of weeks in, I found out that Danny was lying about my work to our manager and making up stories about things that happened in client meetings. He was trying to drag my name through the mud. I was hurt. I only found this information out because our manager brought it to my attention. Our manager asked me about some things that were supposedly taking place in the office, and I quickly said, "No way that has ever happened, nor would I ever do that." We had a hard conversation. My manager was honest with me, and I will never forget it: "Minda, don't worry about the things that Danny is saying. I knew none of what he was insinuating was true because that is not in your character, but as your manager I needed to ask you about it or at least make you aware of it." I was kind of pissed, because I wanted our manager to do something about it. My manager ended with,

"Danny doesn't mean any harm. He has a lot on his plate with his personal life. I am sure he is only doing this because he feels desperate for a leadership position."

I won't sit up here and tell you that I wasn't mad. My manager had more empathy for my lying colleague than for me. I was being asked to be the bigger person. Meanwhile, there were no repercussions for Danny. My manager asked me not to mention anything to Danny regarding our conversation, a conversation that almost made me spiral back into a state of despair. And then I still had to live with Danny for a couple more weeks until my apartment was ready. I sat with the new information, but in my head I drew my line. I knew that I could no longer stay with Danny. For my mental state, I couldn't, as my relatives say, "skin and grin" with him. It was bad enough we had to work together, but I couldn't do it at the crib too. Danny didn't know that I knew about his attempts to discredit me so he could get a promotion. He had said some racialized things about me that really had me questioning the person I had been working and living with. But I couldn't and wouldn't allow him to dismantle a career I was working so hard to build. I continued to work with integrity and grit. And I ended up packing my stuff from his house and staying in a motel. All of my money at that time was wrapped up in the new apartment that wasn't ready yet and the furniture I had just purchased. I didn't have time to get a fancy hotel approved and expensed at that point, and all I could afford out of pocket on such short notice was a two-star motel. But I took the power away from Danny and drew my line in the sand. I knew that I could not stay in his house and play games. Sometimes you have to choose yourself and draw your line. About three months later, I was indeed promoted and got my own contract in a different state, while Danny got left behind. Look at God!

Now, the situation with Danny was a mess. There is no other way to describe it. But what I want to also address is boundary setting and healing when the people you once trusted harm you. Because the reality is, you might be harmed while you are trying to heal. And we don't want that next racialized experience to set you back. That is why I keep sounding like a broken record by providing you with tools you can use when the situation calls for it.

Let's start with boundary setting. With the situation that occurred with my manager and Danny, I made a lot of missteps, and you can probably see what I could have done differently. Often when we are in a situation like this, we tend to be the only woman of color. Many times, we feel like we don't have the agency to have the conversations that need to be had, or we become accommodating at the expense of ourselves. Singer and actress Janelle Monáe said, "Even if it makes others uncomfortable, I will love who I am." And I believe boundaries will require the same thing from you. Drawing your line will sometimes make others uncomfortable, yet you love yourself enough to center yourself in the situation. If I could go back in time and establish boundaries with my manager and with Danny, I would have done it, because I know how critical that would have been to my growth and healing as a Black woman in the workplace.

Even though I was healing from past workplace trauma while being once again racially traumatized, I still could have drawn a line—but I didn't know I could. I want you to know that you can draw your line, because no one else will. Looking back at the situation years later, I no longer blame myself. I learned lessons from that experience.

When things were taking place with Danny, I didn't know he was being a backstabber. Some friends will smile in your face, all the time trying to take your place. I was not made aware of Danny's vicious ways until my manager brought them to my attention. And the first boundary I should have set was when our manager mentioned the lies to me and asked me not to say anything about it. I should have pushed back. Because Danny was in the wrong, but he was being given a pass for bad behavior. Our manager liked Danny. They used to hang out together outside of work. So of course our manager didn't want to deal with it in a real way. I should have required my manager to handle the situation professionally, as a manager and not as Danny's friend. We see this type of behavior all too often inside of the workplace. Social relationships often override ethics, and friendship networks are often racially homogenous. Often, we women of color weren't the ones hired as friends of the boss. And once we are hired, we happen to be the ones who aren't invited to after-work drinks.

My manager had the responsibility to keep all employees psychologically safe but didn't do so. If Danny could easily get a pass for turning on me, and if the manager was maintaining secrecy about this abuse, I could only imagine what other toxic behavior Danny was enacting that colleagues didn't know about. But that is just my assumption.

Even though I wasn't prepared and didn't yet know the full range of options available to me, I did the best I could at the time with the hand I was dealt. Now, some would say that Danny got what he deserved because I ended up getting my promotion and a new contract, but that isn't the point. Yes, in many ways karma met up with Danny, but no one ever required Danny to do anything different. I often think about how many other Black women's emotional well-being was sacrificed by that manager and Danny in the years since.

Another lesson from that experience was that I had to re-think my approach to trusting colleagues in the workplace. Webster's dictionary defines trust as "reliance on the character, ability, strength, or truth of someone or something." Part of our healing will require variations of trust, otherwise we will be side-eyeing every single one of our colleagues, constantly paranoid that they will all someday turn on us. I also understand that it can be hard for healing to take place when trust is fragile. Instead of being mean to Danny, or trying to figure out how to pay him back, or making the workplace awkward for myself and everyone else, I took a different approach. I decided that Danny was a bad egg, yet I didn't have to isolate myself from those in the office who had some integrity. Sometimes when we are hurt, we tend to isolate ourselves and put everyone in the same bag as the person who caused the pain.

I will say, before the Danny situation occurred, I was very naive when it came to workplace friendships. I thought everyone who was nice to me at work was my friend. I hadn't had a lot of professional work experience at this time, and I thought people didn't actually do the foul stuff I saw in TV and in the movies. But, come to find out, some people are indeed that evil. The lessons I learned with Danny were painful, but I needed to know the truth. If I had never been made aware of his deceit, I don't even want to know how that story could have potentially ended. But by the grace of God, I got to see the type of person Danny was. And I was able to be more discerning when it came to getting too close to future colleagues.

Make no mistake, I didn't just slam the proverbial door and say the hell with making work friends, because that mentality would have only hurt my career. I couldn't hold every colleague accountable for Danny's sins, but I was much more aware of how I built relationships in the future. This is a lesson I hope you will take with you on your healing journey. You can't block future allies or good managers due to the bad experiences you've had with others, but moving forward you can be more aware of patterns forming.

One way to know that you are healing is that you won't want to make everyone you work with pay for the racial sins of former or current coworkers. I also learned that some people truly are fair-weather friends; you might not know a person's true character until they start to feel threatened or in competition with you. That was the case with Danny. And if I could go back and do it all over again, I would have diplomatically confronted Danny once I heard what he was doing. I would have asked him about it and got to the bottom of it. For some people, they may decide it's easier to cut others down than to actually do the work of performing better. In that case, having a courageous conversation would not only have been about my own healing, but it would have forced Danny to be honest with me about what he was doing, and maybe that would have helped him think twice before harming other women.

Vibrating Higher

Vibrating higher is my favorite step. There are a few layers to this as you are on your path to healing. You will know healing has started to take place when you are able to vibrate higher—when situations happen and you are unbothered. It doesn't mean they don't bother you at all anymore, because no one likes to be disrespected, but you now know that there are ways you can take back your agency. When you vibrate higher, you will start to ask yourself questions like: Is this the environment that I should be staying in? Is this person's ignorance worth a response? Am I going to let this racial incident take me out of my healing game?

When you vibrate higher, you begin to realize that you don't have to deal with the dumb sh*t anymore and you can start getting your résumé, website, or CV updated. Or perhaps you just walk away from the situation and leave that person trying to figure out why you are no longer engaging with them. When you are vibrating higher, you can't stay too much longer in a toxic environment or entertain certain colleagues, because you are too blessed to stay stressed with these foolish folks.

One example of how I knew I was able to vibrate higher was with a former colleague I'll call Penny. I had worked with Penny for years, and I would say to some degree I knew her fairly well. We didn't hang out outside of work, but we would sometimes grab lunch together or she would catch me up on what her family was up to. Penny would always say some borderline racist stuff, but I just didn't have the energy to always address it. Have you ever been there? In those early days, I was still processing my pain and finding the agency to address that pain.

At one point, Penny told me about her excitement about a family member getting into a fancy college. Well, she was excited except for one thing. Her relative was housing with other students who happened to be Black. And if you hadn't guessed, Penny was white. She went on to tell me a version of her story about how the Black students were being mean to her relative, and she felt like they didn't have proper home training. These students, including Penny's relative, all made it into the same fancy school, so I would imagine they probably had more in common than Penny would like to believe.

I tried my best to be present during the conversation, because at first I thought to myself, *These are just young students who don't know each other experiencing some dorm-room growing pains.* I had some growing pains with my roommate when I moved into my dorm room. Eventually, you settle in, get to know each other, and at least find some mutual respect in a shared space. I wanted to give Penny the benefit of the doubt, but the more she spoke, the more I thought she had an issue with her relative rooming with Black students, because she said they were from the "other side of the tracks." First off, who talks like that anymore? And the last comment she made has been etched in my head ever since. She said, "Minda, why can't Black women be like you? You've done so well at assimilation."

At that moment, I chose to vibrate higher, otherwise I likely would have lost my job. Penny was probably never going to be an ally for me, and she was probably not someone who I would ever see at an equal rights march. I decided

I wasn't going to work myself up for someone who would probably never understand or take responsibility for what she was saying, for being racist and out of line. I would rather spend my healing energy on someone who would learn a real lesson and actually move the equity needle forward. I didn't want to mess up my healing journey for someone like Penny and her racialized words. What I learned in that moment was that it's not my ministry to solve all of Penny's racialized problems. I am not saying there isn't room for her to grow, but I'll be damned if I am going to spend the few free minutes that I have left on my lunch break listening to her call me "assimilated." It's people like Penny who cause so much harm, and they do it with a smile and are rarely questioned. Unfortunately, Penny-type personalities in the workplace run rampant, and it makes it very hard to vibrate higher. But I knew I was healing because I left Penny's racial baggage with her in her cube and I didn't take it with me to mine.

I ended the conversation by saying, "Penny, I will be praying for everyone involved," and I walked away. I couldn't and wouldn't allow her to suck me into being her therapist in that moment while she insulted me at the same time. No ma'am. My decision to vibrate higher was not for Penny, but for me. Because where would I have really gotten with Penny?

What is important about this step is that every racial occurrence no longer sets you off like it might have in the past. This is another situation where boundaries are needed, but vibrating higher goes a step further, as a choice we make to not let every racial situation send us back into a relapse. If you work with a lot of Pennys, then at some point you might decide that in order to stay on your healing journey you need to address those people, leave, or walk away. I just don't want you to think you don't have any options. The one option I don't want you to lean on is always having to subject yourself to their thoughts and feelings at the expense of your own. Vibrating higher is all about the ways we respond emotionally and mentally without completely breaking down. Meaning, if I am in the healing process and I know Penny is being ignorant, I am not going to allow her ignorance to break my peace and my process. I am actively choosing to move forward.

EMBRACE THE PROCESS

Now that I've walked you through all five steps, I'll say again that healing is a process. You'll know you've started healing when you accept that it's not a quick fix. There will be levels to your healing, and your process might be different from mine, but you will undergo your own progression. My Aunt Enako says it best: "As Black women, we sometimes have to go through the process before we reach the reward." During one of our Saturday phone calls, my aunt said, "Part of healing is preparation and strategy, and that requires us not to give up on the process." That is an entire word. I hope you let that marinate in your system just a bit. As you are vibrating higher, it might not always feel good, but you know it's part of your healing process. It will be very hard to heal or know that healing is taking place if you haven't gone through that process.

The best example to bring this home is riding a bicycle. When many of us first learned to ride a bike, we started with training wheels. The training wheels were there to help us learn how to ride. During the process of learning to ride the bike, we learned how to pedal; we also learned how to build our confidence while navigating traffic or people on the sidewalk. Even when we fell over, many of us got back up because we knew that falling would be part of the process. Those falls might have been painful, but we didn't let it stop us from learning to ride the bike. The process wasn't easy, but now you can celebrate because you went through it in your own way. Some learned how to ride a bike without training wheels in a couple of days. Others needed months to learn. We all have a unique process. And that's just like the process of healing. When we are finally able to take those training wheels off and ride like no one is watching, it's a pretty liberating feeling. It's the same with healing and choosing to vibrate higher. We don't have to minimize our power when we feel like we might be falling—we can take it back!

The last thing I want to tell you about these five steps is that they aren't meant to be used as a simple checklist. One or three steps might resonate with you, or perhaps all five. They are meant to help you determine how you can respond to incidents. Then, when you see how you respond the next time, you can evaluate the progress you are making. For example, you might find that you can acknowledge an incident, but you sometimes struggle with deciding what to do about it. In a case like this, you can see the areas that you need to put a little extra focus on. When I was younger, I sometimes used to go with one of my relatives to their Alcoholics Anonymous meetings. One of the principles they would often state is that they will always be in recovery. I feel the same way about my racialized experiences in the workplace; I am always healing and growing. And by allowing myself to heal, I get to pack a little lighter each day.

THE FINAL COUNTDOWN

I couldn't end this chapter without telling you one final story: it's the story I mentioned earlier in the book about almost being brought to my knees. I was on my way to healing, and, lo and behold, here comes some racial BS. I didn't expect it, but we never do. I was already trying to heal from a previous brutal racial assault that almost made me want to give up my career in its entirety. Racism hurts—there are no ifs, ands, or buts about it. It was this next racial episode that surely let me know that healing is a journey, and it might never be a one-and-done type of approach. I am so thankful that I was on my healing journey when this situation struck, because I don't know if I would have been able to bounce back otherwise. I am certain that bitterness would have gotten the best of me.

After I left the East Coast dream job working alongside my abusive coworker Kerry, as you know, I ended up moving on to my next job within thirty days. About two years after being in my new role, I was thriving and performing well. The issue was that I had a series of managers in quick succession. They kept getting poached by other organizations. So every time I would get my footing, here comes a new manager to build a relationship with. As my most recent boss was on her way out, she was grooming me to take over her position. I had no reason in the world to question what she said to me. But when she left, I didn't get promoted into her role, and the powers that be ended up bringing in a gentleman, let's call him James, with way less experience than me and who had a horrible management track record. From what was communicated to me, though, "James is a good guy with a nice wife." Oh, and he was a former TV star. I was furious. I was literally set up for no success. What ended up happening was that he had to rely on me to bring him up to speed.

I was hurt because this was the company's opportunity to diversify the leadership team, and instead they went with someone with less experience. I had to suck it up and try to make it work with James. Almost our entire team was deflated, because folks also thought the manager job was mine. We had all heard what had happened with James's last team, which ended up running for the hills because of his poor management style. Even with all of those facts, James would be my new manager whether I wanted him to be or not. Or at least until I saved enough money to finally leave and run my own business full-time. When I didn't get the promotion, I knew I had to hustle, because I didn't know how long I would be able to work in that type of environment and thrive in my role. I had even spoken to people who I was friendly with at work who had worked for him before, and the reports were never good. I knew I would have to leave at some point. At that time, I was not in a financial position to pack my things and chuck up the deuces. I still needed to build my side business and save like my life depended on it. I told myself to try to make this work for at least another year. *Make work work for you, Minda.* And that is exactly what I attempted to do.

There were many situations that arose with James, unfortunately. He knew that I probably should've had his job and he started to micromanage me and question my every move. He treated me like I was an intern, when I was having one of the most successful job-performance years of my career. Yes, James was annoying as hell, but then he started to sabotage my workplace relationships. I had never had any problems with any of my internal stakeholders until he came aboard and began to interfere. Meetings that I used to have a seat at the table for, he took the lead on, only to have me draft up notes so he could answer questions about my clients. Eventually that didn't work, and the senior leadership asked that I return to my role in running those meetings because he couldn't give as much detailed information as I could—rightfully so.

Was James's treatment racially motivated? I can't honestly answer that question, but I was the only Black woman on the team and he sure seemed to go out of his way to drive me out of my role. Then there was the straw that broke the camel's back. It was the reason I decided to give my notice, because I could no longer work there. I was working on a contract with a high-profile internal stakeholder to potentially hit a performance milestone. I'll call this stakeholder Marla, and we had traveled together for work and become close. We were building a relationship as friends. We weren't the kind of close where we picked up the phone to shoot the breeze, but we were close enough to send a personal text when we needed to communicate about something. When it came to work-related matters, though, I would go through her team for proper protocol, so nothing fell through the cracks.

During a series of conversations, we had planned a VIP reception for some clients we were cultivating relationships with. Through my client connections, we were given seats in a private suite at a playoff game. A very long story short, at one point the connection fell through and we no longer had the suite. I relayed that information to Marla's administrative team, and that was that. About two weeks later, my contact reached back out and said that he got the suite back and gave me some potential dates he could offer me, but he couldn't commit to a specific date so he was holding them all. His company was going through an organizational restructure and he would know more soon. I immediately reached back out to Marla's team and let them know the situation. Her team wrote back and said that Marla would not be able to make any of the dates, but thanks for checking in. I felt like that was the end of it, so I proceeded like I normally would and hosted the group in the suite the next month.

A week after the event, I heard from my manager James, who I had kept in the loop the entire time. He called me and accused me of blocking Marla out and not telling her about the new dates. I was taken aback. I reminded James of the situation and even sent him the email exchanges I had had with her team. He still questioned if I was telling the truth about it. I was so upset with him, because, again, I had kept him in the loop and I gained nothing from hiding the event from Marla. I immediately said that I would call her because we had a relationship. If it turned out that she was available during those dates and she was hurt that she hadn't heard about them, then her team must have dropped the ball. My boss prohibited me from contacting her and asked me to take one for the team, because if I told her the truth then her team would look bad and we needed to keep a good relationship with them.

I pushed back; I didn't like how this picture he wanted to paint made me look. I had the email exchanges to prove that I had communicated clearly with Marla's team. James read them and saw them and chose not to pass them along. He forced me to write her an email with him cc'd and apologize for the nonexistent miscommunication. He actually wanted me to write that I was sorry for cutting her out on the new dates. Basically, he wanted me to lie, but I wouldn't go that far. I closed the email saying that if she had any questions, she could contact me directly. It ended up becoming a huge situation that went up the food chain, and my name was tainted because my manager chose to not have my back. To this day, I don't understand why he didn't stand up for me, why he didn't let me have my own conversations. I even reached out to one of the women on the administrative staff who I had had the last email exchange with, but she was no longer working there.

James then called me into his office and kept pressing me about this issue until I broke into tears. My entire career, I had had the respect of my colleagues, and in a matter of days he had done everything he could to make me look incompetent. He decided to cut me off from other professional relationships. I was prohibited from reaching out to other departments and having my own conversations with people. He claimed that he was the manager and he would speak for me. I had never cried in front of a manager before, but everything from Kerry to now swept over me. Where do all the broken hearts of women of color go when we can't take it anymore? Where do we go when no one stands up for us? Where do we go when no one cares and leaves us to fend for ourselves?

I didn't have the answers, but I knew damn well this Black woman had to go somewhere else. I could no longer work for James.

When I cried in his office, I was disappointed in myself. I felt like I had let the system and James get the best of me. There was no way to pull a Zack Morris and time-out this thing; the tears were in full effect. I was hurt beyond belief. These fools had dropped the ball, and the only Black woman had to take the blame. I said to him that I was disappointed in how he had handled this situation and how he chose not to have my back. He had no words. For a moment, I saw a flicker of empathy. Almost like he was sorry, but he never said it. I am not even sure what was said or wasn't said to Marla, but I never heard from her again.

As a side note, because I can't move on without acknowledging it: James is a bad manager. He was a bad manager before he received his promotion, and I am sure he is still a bad manager because no one required him to be better. I often think about how many people have had to deal with racial trauma under his leadership. I know for myself, even one (me) was one too many. I hate to say it, but I think we often see white managers underperform in the workplace when it comes to addressing racialized situations. Few get training on how to manage racialized incidents, and too many have the instinct of sweeping things under the rug. Sadly, we rarely see any accountability for harm being caused to Black and Brown employees.

Make no mistake, a manager is someone who is supposed to support you and help you do the best work of your career while you are employed there. In James's case, that was not a priority for him. He ended up being the last person I could trust in the workplace. I was constantly questioning if his actions were racially motivated or not. That is something I shouldn't have had to spend my days wondering about. White people will never have to experience that mental anguish— at times the burden seems invisible, and at other times even Mr. Magoo could see that an incident was racialized. If I had not already had some healing tools in my tool kit, I don't know where my mental health would have been after dealing with Kerry and James.

What I know to be true was that James was trying to sabotage me and wanted to see me fail, and that is no conspiracy theory. Workplace abuse should have consequences for the perpetrators. It's one thing when you experience a horrible colleague or someone outside of your department, and it can be even more stressful and painful when you experience harm from your own manager. I saw red flags when James started to isolate me from other departments I had once worked with daily. Another red flag was of course his not having my back or even hearing me out when situations would arise. Instead of removing barriers for me like a good manager should, he created more. As the only Black woman he managed at that time, it's hard not to worry that it was racially motivated.

So what can you do as you heal and deal with managers or colleagues with more senior titles? This situation is quite dangerous during the healing process, because we have to understand that racial workplace trauma will try to break your confidence. And we need our confidence more than ever during the healing process. My advice to you is, first, with any racial workplace issue, please, please document these occurrences with precision. Make sure you have the dates, times, places, and a synopsis written down. I started to blind copy my personal email on every email I sent to James. I didn't trust this guy at all, and I wanted to make sure my paper trail was not tampered with. Second, if you feel comfortable, please call out this behavior. People like James will never admit to the abuse, but at least you did your part. Third, I would ask you to consider filing a complaint with either the EEOC or HR. Again, this is your choice; you have to do what is best for you.

I've had some horrible bosses. I think they might be in competition with any bad boss from a horror movie or perhaps even one that you've experienced yourself. A lot of my workplace pain has been due to managers failing to show up for me when they are supposed to be creating a safe space for all of their team members to succeed, not just the white ones. As I continue to be right within, part of my healing process is to give every new manager an opportunity to build trust with me. I try not to count them out, even though I haven't had the best luck. I do that because it would be too triggering to think that every manager was out to get me. That is not a mindset I can afford to have on my healing journey. Now, don't get me wrong, I keep an eye out for behaviors and patterns that might alert me to similar situations from my past, but I know that I have the power and I don't give it away to people like James. At the end of this book, I have some resources for managers, because I believe they can play a very important role in our healing process if they choose to and if leadership commits to investing in their growth.

I'M OUT OF HERE

Not long after I cried in James's office, I told him that I was giving my notice. I realized that if I was going to continue on my healing journey, I was going to have to leave this environment. Staying there would barely be a survival strategy at that point. I couldn't live in fear because I didn't have the five thousand more dollars I needed to reach my savings-account goal. I would rather piece together random jobs than work another day under this man.

In that moment, I thought back to a woman I used to be friendly with early in my career. Danielle had what some would say was a great job, but she was experiencing an overwhelming amount of racial trauma at work. Eventually, I lost touch with her and ended up seeing her years later working as a cashier. She had left her corporate job because the racism became way too much to handle and eventually started to impact her mental health. When I saw her that day, I had a hard time understanding why she had left corporate America, but I get it now. I understand that she chose her sanity over a paycheck. She chose herself over what others might think. Now I know how much courage that must have taken for her. I will be honest: she seemed way happier as a cashier than she was before.

The day I gave my notice, I immediately felt at peace. That's when I knew that my healing was taking root because I understood I couldn't afford to center anyone else but me.

I realize not everyone can make that decision, but I want you to know that even if bad situations arise and you break down in tears, that doesn't mean you aren't healing. I had to continue to draw upon my faith and know that everything would end up working out, even though I had no idea what things would look like.

And it did end up working out. What you might not know is that a couple of years prior, I had started my company, The Memo LLC, to help women of color navigate the workplace. I knew from my past experiences that women of color don't experience the workplace in the same way as white women, and that was the part of the story that many of us were not saying out loud. I knew there needed to be space where women of color weren't written off as angry, crazy, or making up racism at work. I wanted to remind them there is more in store for them. Six months after I left my job, my first book came out, called *The Memo: What Women of Color Need to Know to Secure a Seat at the Table*, and it became a bestseller. I was able to speak freely about my experiences. I felt like I could set aside some of the obstacles ahead, and the road was becoming a little bit clearer. That probably wouldn't have happened without that step of faith: founding the organization in the first place.

Additionally, I probably wouldn't have started my company if I hadn't realized that I needed to heal from all of my workplace trauma, and that I didn't have to do it alone. As I began to heal from my pain, I started to think about all the other women of color who might benefit from healing as well if they knew it was possible. As you can see, I didn't get every step and process correct, but that didn't stop me from starting my company and sharing my story, not just to benefit me but to benefit us. As I wrote *The Memo*, I experienced even more healing. I often joke that writing my first book was another step in my healing journey. It wasn't until writing *The Memo* that I was able to talk about some of the deepest pains in my career.

While writing this book, I realized that healing has taken place in many areas of my life, but I still have some bruises. Writing this book required me to relive some painful racialized experiences, yet I was able to move through these feelings because I can see that it's all part of my process. I even questioned if I had healed enough to be an authority on healing from racial workplace trauma. What I realized was that I am only an authority on moving through my trauma, but if my story of healing can help other women of color, then it is worth telling. We can't get to our healing if we don't go through our process. I pull my strength from knowing that we are so much stronger when we show up together as our best selves, free of the racial terrors that have tried to hold us back. Articulating that and owning it is a form of healing.

Another lesson I learned from past racial workplace trauma is that I needed to go back and deal with it all. I could no longer compartmentalize my racial trauma. I needed to heal from every part of the pain, not just from Kerry and James, but anybody else who had caused me harm. I deserved to be free from all the racial trauma, and it is important for me to remind you that you deserve that as well. If you didn't know by now, your healing is a revolutionary act. Can you imagine how free we will be, showing up in the world healed and whole? I am excited about that day. The workplace better watch out.

THE JOURNEY CONTINUES

Right now, you still might be questioning if you are healing or regressing. Again, there is no timeline for healing. My only hope is that you continue to remain open to exploring what healing could look like and understanding what healing pathways are available to you so you can live your best life. There might be days when you feel hopeless, and there will be other days when you pat yourself on the back because you know you are making progress. Those progress days will help you keep moving toward your finish line. Just don't forget to keep your faith, even when you don't see it or feel it. Trust the process.

When the racialized situation happened with Kerry, I felt defeated, broken, and unsure of myself. I didn't have the tools I needed to heal or deal with the situation in a healthy manner. As you could see, in my next workplace situation I was met with another blow from my manager James. But the good news is that some healing had taken root, so that even though I cried in James's office, I was much stronger than I was before. At that moment, I didn't see myself as strong. But looking back, I held James accountable and I articulated my truth to him. I knew I was healing because it wasn't about James or about whether he would apologize. I was strong enough to handle the situation myself. I didn't leave my job because I thought I didn't have any other option; I left because my healing was too important to me and staying would have hurt me in the long run. My mindset had completely shifted from my Kerry days to my James days.

Another difference was that I requested an exit interview when I left my last employer, that is something I didn't do when I left the workplace with Kerry. I wanted to make sure that I stamped my voice and my experience onto my former company. I wanted my healing footprint to be left, in case someone else needed some support when they experienced James as a manager.

As I continue to heal, I am aware of the triggers and patterns, and I use my tools and frameworks when I need some reinforcements. I told you the story about the feelings I used to have when I would fly in first class. I could feel some of my fellow passengers and the flight attendants judging me. Now I know I belong, and I am not beholden to racist ideologies of who gets to sit in the back or the front of the bus. I no longer give thought to what the lady across the aisle is thinking when she sees me sit down. Or when the person next to me talks to me as if this is my first time in first class and treats me like some child at Disneyland by telling me I can order whatever I want. Those moments can definitely be triggering, but I don't let them paralyze my healing and my growth. Yes, they might wonder why I am there, but, frankly my dear, I don't give a damn. Sometimes part of our healing is not giving any damns about certain things that used to bring us to our knees, because we know how to navigate and address them now.

The writer Zora Neale Hurston once said, "Sometimes, I feel discriminated against, but it does not make me angry.

It merely astonishes me. How can any deny themselves the pleasure of my company? It's beyond me." I truly feel that we will know that healing has taken root when we have the same or similar outlook as Ms. Hurston. I won't say that when you experience a racialized moment in the workplace it won't hurt anymore, yet I would ask you to consider finding ways you can take the power back from the Kerrys and Jameses and Pennys and their hurtful words. I believe it's possible to continue our healing and find ways to stay empowered on our journeys.

One thing to keep in mind is that we will encounter so many people like these bad colleagues and managers, but at some point we can decide that they are being ignorant, racist, and a host of other things and they are only shrinking themselves with their own racism. We don't have to let their ignorance weaken, shrink, or prevent us from healing.

Time to Unpack and Reassess

1. You have journeyed through a few chapters, and I am curious: What does healing mean to you now?
2. How are you finding ways to keep up with your mental hygiene?
3. What steps from RMF resonate most with you?
4. Are there areas where you are seeing healing take root?

Chapter 6

MAINTENANCE

And when it seems that I'm hopeless
You say the words that can get me back in focus
—2Pac, "Dear Mama"

The civil rights and voting rights activist Fannie Lou Hamer coined the phrase "We're tired of being tired." Ms. Hamer was referring to racism. Women from past generations implemented strategies to help them fight for their place in this world, despite the ugly truths of discrimination, segregation, and sexism. They probably would have given up a long time ago, but they incorporated healing strategies like singing hymns, starting social clubs, and attending church to help them feel grounded on the days when it might have felt too hard to fight for their rights. They knew they might never eradicate racism in their lifetimes, yet they still had to find joy on those stormy nights.

Women like Fannie Lou Hamer had to incorporate strategies to help them not give up when their homes were burned down. They had to integrate systems when they were beaten at the voting booths for trying to cast their ballots for the first time. Because without those strategies, they might have lost their minds. They knew they might not be able to cut off racism's head, and they knew that, even if they did, it might eventually grow back. They knew that racism was always waiting in the brush to attack, yet they had their tools in place to stand up against racist systems and oppressive behaviors. They began to take authority over those systems and not let racism and their foot soldiers have power over them.

TRYING TO MAINTAIN

Just as they incorporated and created strategies to keep moving forward, we need maintenance strategies to preserve our healing in these work environments that still have racist people and systems at the helm. Maintenance is required if we don't want to experience racialized relapse continuously. The word "relapse" is defined as "a deterioration in someone's state of health after a temporary improvement." We might improve or move on and experience a form of healing from one workplace to another—and if that happens, what a difference a new workplace can make. But there might be racialized systems of oppression in your new workplace too. Then what are you going to do?

The last thing I want is for you to experience a relapse in your healing in each new environment. And I don't say that to be cynical or to speak something negative over your life, because I would never do that. I want you to experience nothing but goodness in your career. But I know that some of our oppressors have not received their healing, and wounded people can sometimes wound other people. You have worked too hard to allow them to stop you from your healing finish line. The ugly truth of American culture is that racism might not die in our lifetimes, and when we are near it, we have to have our guardrails in place so those systems don't derail us on our path to wholeness.

Maintenance will be required because some colleagues will say some out-of-pocket stuff. After all, that is who they are. There will be managers who don't advance you because they can't see themself in you. And there will be those in the workplace who will call you the wrong name and mistake you for the other woman of color who looks nothing like you. We will all have those days. I wish I could tell you that once you've healed from past workplace trauma you will never be faced with its oppressive systems again, but that is not the world we live in. The reality is that some coworkers will never change their behaviors because their privilege reminds them that they don't have to. When we understand oppressive systems and behaviors, we can find those strategies to maintain our healing when we are met with racialized situations.

GIVE YOURSELF TIME

Please allow me to put the power of maintenance into perspective for you. When I left my position working with Kerry, thirty days later I had a new job. After that racialized experience, I was so emotionally fragile that I didn't realize

I hadn't given myself enough time before starting a new job. Don't get me wrong—praise be to God that I could escape my racially abusive environment, but I exited with bags full of trauma. And with all that trauma, I had the nerve to start a new work relationship. Why don't we look at the workplace like any other relationship? If I had been leaving a romantic relationship, you would be like, *Oh, Minda, I think you need to lie low for a minute before dating again.* And you wouldn't be wrong. If a past lover had just terrorized me, I probably wouldn't be the best partner running into someone else's arms. I would more than likely be nervous, anxious, and triggered by things that reminded me of my last relationship. And I probably wouldn't be able to bring my whole self to my new relationship because I hadn't reconciled some of the things from my past. A toxic work relationship will have you experiencing all of those emotions and more.

Now I understand that everyone doesn't have the luxury of sitting things out and healing completely before finding or starting a new job. And that's precisely why maintenance is so essential. I want us to have a real conversation around our maintenance strategies. We will need some additional tools to keep up with our healing while working in these various environments. Because the reality is, racism isn't going anywhere anytime soon. If we don't adapt or create systems within our lives to heal through the trauma, we will continue to pick up that trauma instead of learning to release it. I wasn't able to be right within and pack light because I felt married to my trauma. In some weird way, it had become part of me. Erykah Badu told us that all them bags gonna get in our way if we don't pack light. And let me tell you, them bags indeed started to get in my way.

DON'T TAKE THEM WITH YOU

My brain and body started to react to new racialized experiences that would set me back on some days. There were days at my new job when I felt like I was waiting around for Kerry to email me with some nonsense because most of my old workdays were filled with anxiety via my inbox. I was nervous to even read some of the emails from my new coworkers because of my anxiety, which is crazy, because Kerry no longer worked with me. Yet I was still carrying that trauma.

I even remember sitting in the lobby of a Fortune 500 company to see a client and wondering what I would do if Kerry were to walk in. I would create a scenario in my mind starring Kerry and costarring yours truly. I would go down this rabbit hole of asking myself, *Would I cuss her out, would I pretend I didn't know her, or would I run out crying?* I was living in fear. I was so shook you would have thought I had seen a ghost. And this was all taking place in my mind. Boy oh boy, I wish I could go back and give myself some maintenance strategies for that time. I was in the process of trying to find healing, but it was hard because I had packed all my Kerry-related pain inside one of my bags and brought them to this new place. I was still holding onto past bags, and I didn't allow myself to be free. This is precisely why we have to continue to pack light. Do you know that you have the power to release yourself from your racialized past? You don't have to spend all day, every day haunted by your past. Once I realized that I possessed the power of healing, I was able to start intervening on my behalf.

When I started my new job, I was susceptible to my new colleagues' language and tone. My last environment was racially toxic, and some of the things my new colleagues would say made me feel uncomfortable. It started to become hard for me to decipher who truly meant well and who didn't. I was constantly tormented by what may or may not have been accurate. It compounded my racialized trauma in hard-to-articulate ways, yet I imagine you might know exactly how I felt because you might have experienced or are currently experiencing this kind of feeling. What I don't think we talk enough about is workplace paranoia and emotional scars. Often, we only attribute abusive situations in a romantic or parental context, yet harm or abuse can take place in a work relationship, be it verbal, emotional, or physical. Workplace abuse is just as insidious as any other form of abuse.

I am sure you've heard people say, "Don't take it personally" or "This is only business. Keep the emotions out of it." Both statements are problematic, because people bring themselves to work, and as a human being you will feel certain emotions when someone is treating you with respect and others when someone is disrespecting you. Some may see workplace abuse in the abstract, yet those racial slights are very serious to the person on the receiving end. It's almost like our white colleagues believe that racism only happens on the streets, or with the police, or in the South. But women of color know that racism happens in the workplace, and it happens by the minute. It happens when our manager speaks down to us, it happens when colleagues make jokes at our expense, and it happens when no one bothers to acknowledge Black History Month. The worst of it is, when a woman of color attempts to speak on it or goes to someone in power who she thinks might be able to help, she is met with someone who won't hold the wrong-doers accountable and just sends her right back to work with her abusers. She is asked to give it another try to make it work. Instead, what should be happening is some managerial coaching, on-site therapy, and at the very least some accountability.

There aren't too many things I hate in this world, but the normalization of workplace harm is one that I will never stop speaking truth to power on. If you are a white person reading or listening to this book, for a moment, just think about how burdensome this trauma is for women of color and the paranoia we carry around with us every day at work. In July 2002, Roderick Kramer wrote about "prudent paranoia" in a *Harvard Business Review* article called "When Paranoia Makes Sense." He wrote about the moderate forms of suspicion that many employees experience because trust has been broken inside of the workplace. Kramer says, "Prudent paranoia is a form of constructive suspicion regarding the intentions and actions of people and organizations."

I started to think about how prudent paranoia is something that many women of color experience at work. We might feel it when a colleague leaves us off the meeting agenda, or our manager never calls on us in the meeting. Or we may have been burned so many times that now we aren't even sure who we can trust at work. Kramer goes on to describe how this type of paranoia might make people feel: "The more we worry, the more we notice. And the more we notice, the more we worry."

What we know to be true is that any form of paranoia can be paralyzing, especially if you are a woman of color in the workplace. Sometimes the self-doubt and questioning of our trauma is a continuous cycle. Even though the workplace should be held accountable, we will have to be accountable for our own healing. But I never want you to doubt that this harm is a big deal. As we allow ourselves the space to heal along our journey, together let us never normalize workplace abuse of any kind.

TRIGGER-HAPPY

As we work toward maintaining our healing, it's important we understand what our emotional triggers are. I mention this to you because there will always be triggers. And when those racialized triggers happen, there will be times when you will have to intervene on your own behalf. During a personal intervention, Superman will not come and save you; you will be tasked with saving yourself and being your own hero. Let's explore what this looks like. Let's say one of your colleagues or managers says the following statements to you:

- Don't take it personally.
- You're so articulate.
- That's just Tom being Tom.
- Assume good intentions.
- You misunderstood what I meant.

Any of these five statements could send us straight through the roof. The language and tone are dismissive and, more times than not, a person of color is on the receiving end. When you experience these statements, what will you do to maintain your peace of mind and well-being? Or will they cause you to relapse? Now, there is no judgment or right answer. But we can't fool ourselves into thinking that just because our colleagues went through some unconscious-bias training that they've been redeemed from racism and prejudice. I can tell you to have grace and extend empathy when they do or say some wild stuff, but the reality is, you have to center yourself and put guardrails up for when these things happen. Because if you don't you might spiral back and pick up some bags that you dropped off years ago.

I don't want any of us letting these workplace oppressors dictate how long our healing lasts or if we achieve recovery at all. We have to continue healing despite their ignorance. That's why I think it's important to incorporate personal intervention strategies for when these situations arise. Let's take a look at how this might work in real time. For example, your colleague says, "Sandra, you are so articulate. I just can't believe it. Where did you grow up?"

Now, for my readers who are not of color, you might read this statement and see nothing wrong with it. Let me put you up on game. We, Black women and other women of color, hear these racial aggressions our entire lives. You might make these statements with the assumption that your Latina or Asian American colleague couldn't have grown up in the United States with English as her native language. Or with the idea that Black people don't know how to speak proper English, like being articulate is a superpower that many Black people never attain. You know when you make statements like you can't hire a person of color because you "don't want to lower the bar"? Well that is some racist BS. And when you say it, it drives us mad. Allow yourself to humanize this statement. What if someone always acted surprised whenever they commented that you spoke well? It would be annoying, right? Okay, I just wanted to make sure we are on the same page before moving on.

So, for readers of color, if this is the millionth time hearing these comments, you might have hit your *Snapped* moment. And that is what I don't want you to do—*snap*. You might need a personal intervention because, if you snap, you are going to be hard on yourself or say something you'll regret, and I am not encouraging you to do that. Remember when I mentioned the part about paranoia? If we keep hearing racialized comments from a colleague, at some point it's no longer paranoia. That person believes we don't belong and doesn't care that their othering is harming us. That is why we have to maintain our healing and protect our peace. Maintaining your healing during challenging times in the workplace boils down to how you problem-solve. This problem-solving centers you; it is not meant to find solutions that benefit your racist coworkers. Our mental health matters, and I hope that more of our employers will realize that as well. They not only need to understand that this harm is not productive, but they actually need to do something tangible about eradicating this racial behavior.

WHATCHU GONNA DO?

In the example that I used, what could maintenance look like if you were in that situation? Let's investigate this situation further through four key elements.

1. Their Intent

We must first understand the intent behind the comment. Was it the first time our colleague or manager said this to us? Or are these microaggressions happening daily? Are they saying things like this just to us, or to other people of other backgrounds?

The baseline is that they shouldn't have said it, period, so that is something we don't even have to debate. With that said, I have been around people who have said certain things, but I don't think they meant harm. I believe they were ignorant. On the other hand, we can't make up this narrative that people do horrible things and no one ever means any harm. At some point, those inflicting harm have to own it. We have to understand the difference between the two. Because when we understand the intent, we can be a better problem-solver and find a solution that suits our healing needs. Regardless of whether that person meant to harm, we still need to address the pain. And we can no longer give out hall passes for good intentions if it always makes us feel lousy.

2. Now, Later, or Never

This is a vital part of our intervention process. Do you feel like you want to address this now? Do you feel like you want to address it later? Or do you feel like you will never handle it? I mentioned it before, and I will repeat it: we have choices. And we have an option to hold that person accountable. If you address it now, what might that look like? If you handle it tomorrow or at the end of the week, what would that look like? In the end, you might decide that addressing this situation isn't where you want to use your energy, and you might put it in your mental files. At the very least, you are aware of how this person likes to get down, so you can choose to stay clear of them. There is no right or wrong way. Yet I do believe that if we never address these racialized situations, that person will blithely continue to oppress people who look like us in the workplace.

My belief is that to dismantle systems of oppression in the workplace, we will have to have critical conversations. These folks need to know their words and actions bother us. Whitney Houston raised an excellent point: "How will I know?" And I ask you a similar question: "How will they know?" If we always choose never to say anything, they won't ever learn their lesson. Part of our healing has to include making them aware of what harms us.

3. Self-Talk

You are aware of your triggers. If someone says something racist or otherwise bigoted, often it wasn't the first time you've heard someone say it. Unfortunately, it might not be the last. So what do you need to tell yourself in the moment to be all right? What are you going to do to make sure you don't relapse and pick up that raggedy old trauma tote bag? I would consider telling myself, *I am not their words.* It might sound simple, but when we've heard their harmful language for hours, days, years, and decades, we have to remind ourselves that we aren't the identities they project onto us based on their limited understanding of our race, ethnicity, or orientation.

When those from the dominant majority do and say things that leave us feeling uncertain about our progress on our healing journey, we must remind ourselves that we are not who they say and think we are. Your identity as a Black, Brown, Indigenous, or trans woman has nothing to do with their words. They created their words to be oppressive and to stop us from living an abundant life at work and in the world. Bigotry was meant to box us in, and we can't live within their box. My identity, your identity, is not the angry, feisty, or docile person they keep trying to project on us. Their ideas of your racial identity don't have to be your lived identity. That is why understanding our triggers is key, so we can have our healing tools ready to go when we need them and we don't have to waste time fumbling around trying to find them.

4. Let It Go

Elsa was onto something when she sang, "Let it go" and "turn away and slam the door / I don't care what they're going to say." Real talk. Whether you decide to address the situation or do nothing about it, once you've decided, let it go! Because the last thing we need you to do is play those scenes over and over again on a reel in your mind. You can't play that song "Shoulda Woulda Coulda" on repeat. It doesn't serve us at all when we do that. When we start to internalize a bad situation, nothing good ever comes of it. It's like tossing around a Ping-Pong ball of racial aggressions in your mind with no escape, further undoing your healing. You have to have your NeNe Leakes moment—"I said what I said"—and be done with it.

If you decide to ruminate on what was said, trying to figure out what you might have said to bring about the microaggression and obsessing over how it could have been avoided, you are picking up that centering-whiteness bag all over again. You don't have to let that incident keep you up each night. You didn't ask them to harm you. This isn't your fault. I get it; if blaming yourself is a bad habit, it can be a hard one to unlearn. But you only have one life to live, so be bold and beautiful or you will be left young and restless, and you deserve better as the world turns.

While I was transitioning into my new job, I was suffering from my past racial trauma and about to enter into some new racialized experiences. Now that I look back on some of those racialized moments, that song "Never Would've Made It" by Marvin Sapp rings so true for me. There's a line that goes, "When I look back over all you brought me through / I can see that you were the one I held on to." Whew! I know for a fact that my faith in God was what got me through those next racialized moments without completely spiraling into a place of despair. I know it wasn't due to my strength. I am equally thankful for my therapist, because she had given me some tools to process and I had created some of my own along the way, which I have shared in this book. Don't be afraid to create some of your own along the way too.

IT'S WORKING TOGETHER FOR MY BENEFIT

Maintenance strategies really can make or break your healing progression. I remember attending a working lunch with an executive at my office; let's call him Keith. I was staffing him for an important client meeting to close a significant deal. I considered this executive a good and decent man, and we got along great. I had no reason to think that he didn't have my back. But then again, we had never been in a situation that would require him to have my back. At any rate, we sat down for lunch and waited on the clients, who were running about ten minutes late.

The clients were a married couple. The husband, John, was a white male, and the wife, Connie, was a woman of color. I had spent time with Connie before, and we had a good rapport. I had met John briefly but had never spent any real time with him. To make a long story short, another Black man had been murdered by the police recently and the story was dominating the news, and somehow it came up in conversation. At one point during lunch, John said, "I just don't get it. Why has it taken Black people so long to get themselves together? I mean, look what happened with the Japanese, and they have been able to accomplish so much."

My mouth dropped to the floor, like, *Dude, you know I am part of those "Black people" you speak of.* I was beyond surprised, and I could see Connie and Keith trying to look away while John proceeded to keep his foot in his mouth.

Before I knew it, I said, "I disagree. You can't compare the hundreds of years of racial oppression that Black people have faced in this country to Japanese people's experiences in this country. Yes, they've experienced racial bias, yet many of those families received a form of reparations as well." But clearly John was trying to pit one group who was oppressed by white people against another, which in my opinion is an anti-Black position.

I remember taking a sip of water and saying an internal prayer that Connie would stop this jerk or that Keith would chime in. But neither of them said a mumblin' word. They let him continue to inflict his ignorance of Black people on the only Black person sitting at the table. If my face could turn red, I am sure that it would have. At that point, I was determined not to go back and forth with this fool who had been sleeping during all of his history classes. I ended the conversation with, "Maybe this is a conversation we should save for dinner and drinks." I awkwardly laughed and shifted the topic back to the reason we were at lunch in the first place.

After lunch, I was riding in the car with Keith and secretly hoping that he might say something about what had transpired. But, yet again, he was a colleague who couldn't or wouldn't step up when I needed him. His stop came first, and when he got out of the car, I felt tears well up in my eyes. I was triggered. Keith might as well have put me back in the office with Kerry. For some reason, I expected more from him. But then again, why did I? I wanted to give him the benefit of the doubt. I wanted him to see me in that moment and feel what I felt. I wanted him to care. Also, I wanted to believe that Keith was different than my former colleagues, who watched the racialized situations go down and did nothing. It's because of situations like this and others that I had to incorporate maintenance strategies. Because my day doesn't end after someone says some BS. I still have to continue to work, take care of my family, and be present. I had to learn not to allow those racialized experiences to paralyze the rest of my day. I refused to let racism have power over me anymore.

Later that evening, I met back up with Keith for a dinner with some of our clients—not John and Connie, thank God. We both arrived early to chat about our game plan for the dinner. When I was in the situation with Kerry, I hadn't advocated for myself in the ways that I wanted to due to fear. This time, I got the courage to casually bring up the situation that had transpired at lunch. I asked Keith what he thought about what John had said. He seemed surprised that I had brought it up and replied, "Well, you know, I am sure he didn't mean any harm."

When he said those words, I felt like Ralph Kramden from *The Honeymooners*. I wanted to take Keith straight to the moon. For the love of God! That man had the audacity to eat his lunch that we paid for and look me straight in the eye and make the case that Black people could have had a better shot at the American dream but didn't work as hard as the Japanese. And Keith had the nerve to tell me he didn't mean any harm? *What the hell did John mean then, Keith?*

Sigh! At that point, I was starting to get upset all over again, so I decided to drop it. One of my maintenance strategies is not letting go of my good energy. I knew that if I allowed myself to relapse in that moment, it would ruin my entire evening. I didn't want to let ignorance and racism take away my positivity.

We have a choice. Don't ever let them try to convince you that we don't. We can choose to prioritize our mental health, even when others won't. And I had more choices still. I could have chosen to either bring it up or leave it alone. We also have the choice to let those moments fester or release them.

I felt proud of myself that I even brought it up to Keith, be-cause I wouldn't have taken that step in the past. I would have let everyone off the hook. Letting people off the hook was a coping strategy back then, because I didn't think I had the agency to center myself and my feelings. Even though Keith didn't want to admit that John was wrong, like Big-gie said, they were both "dead wrong." I knew they were, and I no longer needed someone else to confirm that racism was taking place. My word was enough. That was another maintenance strategy for me: knowing and owning that my feelings make the situation valid. You don't need anyone else to validate your experience.

When I experienced the situation with John, Connie, and Keith, I used darn near all of my personal intervention strat-egies, numbers two through four. But ultimately, I decided to let it go. I let it go after I addressed the parts of the racial harm that I felt needed to be addressed. I light-weight ad-dressed them with John at lunch, and I brought them up to Keith before our last client dinner of the day. I knew in my heart that I would never receive an apology from any of those people. It would have been nice to have, but I couldn't allow myself to ruminate on how they didn't show up for me.

Allowing myself to focus on the lack of allyship is partly why it took me so long to heal from the Kerry situation I have told you so much about. One of my triggers is colleagues who I thought were work friends, but who never showed up as a friend when I needed them to. With John, Connie, and Keith, I had experienced a lack of support a few times in less than twenty-four hours. If I had experienced a day like that years earlier, it would have probably sent me over the edge.

Man, I used to spend so much energy ruminating and replaying scenarios over and over and over again. What I have learned through my healing journey is that rumination and loss of my time and energy is the most dangerous place for me, and it interferes with my healing path forward.

As you continue on your journey, you will identify what those areas are for you as well. Additionally, I used my self-talk to remind myself that I can show up for myself. And that is exactly what I did. I continue to show up for myself in those racial moments in the workplace. I know that I am my own superhero, and any additional help would just be icing on the cake.

BYE FELICIA

About a month later, Connie called me on the telephone. I wanted to believe that she was calling to apologize for her husband and for sitting there like a bump on a log. Of course, she did not even bring it up. She was calling to ask me for a favor for a friend of a friend. This time, I had to count to ten, because this lady was part of my last racialized moment, and now she was asking me to do something for her when she was not capable of showing up for me. This is why humanizing the workplace is so important.

I chose to stay professional and keep the conversation going in a work-related manner. This is another time I had to use my personal maintenance strategies to avoid relapse and stay in a state of wellness. Because these folks will work your last nerve if you let them. At the end of our call, she asked if I wanted to meet up for lunch, and I declined.

We can take our power back. We don't have to pretend, we don't have to put on a performance, and if we don't want to teach, we don't have to do that either. Always choose yourself and your healing. I did enjoy past lunches with Connie, but she and I knew that what her husband said was not cool and I refused to kiki with her like everything was all good. I don't have to subject myself to people like Connie. People like her are just as bad as John.

Stephen Covey said it best: "I am not a product of my circumstances. I am a product of my decisions." We don't have to be a product of others' racial insults, aggressions, or biases. Yet we can produce the outcomes that we want based on how we decide to handle our workplace racialized experiences. We can't dictate how the person giving out the racialized insult handles it, but we can and must continue to center our feelings, because our lives depend on it. To be honest, people like John will probably never change. And those aren't the people we should spin our wheels over. We just have to put people like him on our prayer list and keep it moving.

ZONES OF TOLERANCE

One important element of maintenance is understanding your pain points, as I mentioned in Chapter 1. Each of us process trauma differently, so please don't compare your pain, healing, or reaction to anyone else's. The way that some things might trigger or traumatize you is unique to you. So when people say stupid things like, "You're taking things the wrong way," there is no such thing. Your feelings are valid 24-7. I would like to present to you what I call the Zones of Tolerance. These zones are on a gradient, from comfort to growth to danger. When you feel triggered in the workplace, please use these zones as an additional tool to help you healthily process your trauma. You can have a range of responses to a range of incidents, and wherever you are on the gradient, your feelings are valid. Knowing what responses are available to you can help you work through the pain, and that externalization can help you heal. We don't want you to hoard all of that trauma inside of your body or mind.

Racialized occurrences in the workplace can be painful. I think it's safe to say that we all understand what pain is, but do you know what you can tolerate at work on a good day versus when you have reached your threshold? I almost wish there was a button at each of our desks and, when we've had enough micro- and macro-aggressions for the day, we hit the orange button and that means don't approach me, and please don't say sh*t else to me today. But in the real world, we don't have that button yet, so I can only offer you this spectrum of responses to help you address some of the tension. Let's take an example and work through the various zones to show how this tool might work for you.

Let's say it's 8 a.m. on a Monday and one of your colleagues decides to schedule a last-minute video conference call. During the call, you choose not to turn your video on because your baby was up all night, and your electricity went out due to a storm, and you couldn't blow-dry your hair. Midway through the call, your colleague Max (white, male) says, "I guess Jamie is too hungover to join the rest of us on this morning's call. You people sure know how to party after a big sporting event." Then, at 11 a.m. you receive a call from Doug (white, male), asking for your advice on how to approach Kortney because she seems "unapproachable," and he figured you might have some insight (you and Kortney are the only Black women in the office). Lastly, as the workday is nearing an end, you receive an internal email congratulating Ryan (white, male), who is less accomplished than you are and who started at the company after you did, on his promotion. Both you and Ryan applied for the job, and now the company has added their fifth white man to the executive suite.

1. Comfort
   - In this zone, you are fine with the current situation and you don't think what has transpired is racially motivated. This is where you don't have to spend any extra emotional energy because you are comfortable with what you have just experienced.
   - Additionally, you understand that not every negative or positive situation in the workplace is racially motivated.

2. Growth
   - A question to ask yourself: When a racialized situation occurs, is this an area where I still have some healing to do?
   - You are committed to growing through the pain that you might experience. Even though you are feeling some discomfort, you will use your tools and grow through the moment and not regress.
   - As you continue to heal, you feel the need to have conversations with your colleagues in a productive manner to express your concern about how you

would like to engage going forward, so that this situation doesn't take place in the future.

3. Danger
   • In this zone, you realize the situation is completely triggering and you might need to rely on your healing tool kit right away.
   • You are acknowledging that you are overwhelmed and not in a good place emotionally.
   • Even though you are feeling triggered, you are reminding yourself that your healing is important and you will fight for it.
   • You are feeling like you might not be able to bounce back from this and your tolerance is shaky.

Some white readers might wonder if it's realistic to imagine that many microaggressions in a day. But too many readers of color know some of our days can be filled with all of this nonsense and more.

Now, as women of color, we may respond differently to days like this. One woman might say she is in the comfort sphere with Ryan receiving the promotion because she is giving her colleagues the benefit of the doubt, and perhaps he had some other accomplishments that she wasn't aware of. Another woman might say she is in the growth sphere related to Ryan, because she wanted that promotion too, yet she is choosing to redistribute her energy elsewhere. A third woman might be in the danger zone by the end of the day after a series of incidents like that. *Hand me that orange button!* And another woman might say, *Well, this morning's call*

put me in the danger zone, past the point of no return, after what
Max said.

Again, some of these situations might be triggers for one woman of color and have no real effect on another, and neither person is right or wrong; it's your personal Zone of Tolerance. The point I want to make is that we can monitor where we are when a racialized or potentially racialized situation occurs, which will be important if you decide to focus on maintaining your healing.

If I put myself in the situation with Max, then I would be in the danger zone. Max's harmful and non-inclusive language would more than likely play on a loop in my head, and I would spend half the day annoyed because Max had no idea why I was not on video. He took the liberty of peddling his false narrative while trying to be cute. This situation in particular would be triggering for me because of all my past traumatizing racial experiences. If a colleague racially assaults me in public and none of my colleagues show up for me, then this is a potentially dangerous place for a relapse for me. I have to make sure I use my various healing tools so I don't allow myself to stay in the danger zone.

I also need to understand what my triggers are so I know what to do next, which is critical. I refuse to let anyone stop me from my goals of career health and wellness. After all the work I have put in to get to this point in my healing journey, I'll be damned if I let someone stunt my progress and growth. I've worked too hard to lean out now.

When you find yourself in the danger zone, I would like you to consider using some affirmations to help you maintain your well-being. Use them in a way that doesn't sweep what was said or done under the rug but centers how you're feeling in the moment. Please feel free to create your own affirmations as well. I'm just offering a few examples:

- I am acknowledging that I am not in a good place right now and I don't feel psychological safety.
- I have a choice to have a courageous conversation with those who have racially insulted me. This conversation would be for my benefit. Even if they don't say what I need to hear, I am affirming my voice and my feelings and centering myself in the workplace.
- I choose not to allow this situation to stunt my progress or continue to produce trauma in my life because of others' ignorance and bigotry.
- I choose to move toward a zone of growth.
- I choose me.

It is important to affirm ourselves when we don't have others who affirm us as well, and affirming yourself can be healing and soothing. We shouldn't pretend like nothing took place. These affirmations acknowledge the harm and can provide you with empowering self-talk when you need it.

I hope that you will eventually create your own affirmations and take it one step further, perhaps creating a self-talk script that can help you prepare for when those racial occurrences arise. You might consider a script you can use when racial incidents occur via electronic correspondence, video, phone, or in person. Don't be afraid to create talking points and affirmations that are more authentic to your voice. As you begin to think about writing your own affirmation statements and scripts, I wanted to give you a visual affirmation to help center yourself in racialized moments of touch-and-go.

The lotus flower is considered one of the most sacred plants in the world. In many Eastern cultures, the lotus flower has significant meanings, including rebirth and spirituality. According to the popular blog *Balance by Buddha Groove*, in the Buddhist religion, the lotus flower is a representation of "a journey from a muddy seed to a glorious blossom." Meaning, beautiful things can grow from suffering, and we can be reborn. The same can be true when it comes to healing; we are like lotus flowers. Others might hurt us, but we can come back better than ever because of the healing in our lives. Not only that, through affirmations, we remind ourselves where our strengths lie or what we are good at, especially when someone tries to discount what we bring to the table. There is so much negativity to be absorbed in the workplace that the stories and words we tell ourselves will help remind us who we are and why being right within is so important. Some might say that healing is corny, but I'd rather be thriving with my affirmation statements than suffering without any. Healing is a practice, not a one-time event.

SUCCESS IS NOT A SOLO SPORT

The last part of the maintenance puzzle that I want to tell you about is making sure you have a squad of people who can help you stay on your healing journey. Our healing success won't be a solo sport. We have discussed faith leaders and therapists who might be part of your healing regimen, but who are the other people in your life who can be part of your healing treatment plan? I have asthma, and I use a rescue inhaler to keep my asthma under control on those days when my allergies are impacted by pollen or whenever I work out too hard. I know to never leave home without my inhaler. I might not have an asthma attack, but I don't want to be without my treatment if I need it. Please treat your healing from racialized trauma in the workplace the same way.

I recommend having two kinds of people as part of your treatment plan: a *healing advisor* and a *champion*. A healing advisor and a champion are not the same as your faith leader or therapist. Your faith leader or therapist might be on your speed dial, but advisors and champions can be added to the squad.

A healing advisor is someone you trust, who might be a friend, partner, or relative. When you can't get Jesus on the main line, this is the person who can talk you off the edge until Jesus calls you back. We don't have to suffer in silence. I can tell you there were some days when I had to leave the physical building and call my mom because I needed her to pray with me or tell me to go back in there and finish the day with my head held high. It's nice to know you don't have to battle through the day alone. A healing advisor is someone on the outside of your situation who can offer you encouragement or guidance when you are experiencing trauma or feeling triggered.

Additionally, I would encourage you to have a champion, someone who is on the inside of the workplace with you. They don't necessarily have to be in the same department, but they should be someone you trust to bounce ideas off of or perhaps someone you can ask to show up for you when the situation calls for it. This might be another colleague who has been in meetings when Max has said a racially offensive comment. Let your champion know what you need them to do the next time Max says something offensive. Or, if they felt courageous enough, they could speak to Max about being more aware of the non-inclusive language he is using. The internal champion is critical. I also understand you might not have someone on the inside who can serve in this way but try to find someone. Like I said, even if they are in another department, you will feel more supported in those situations.

When I was dealing with my Kerry situation, there wasn't anyone on my team who would stick their neck out for me in public. They only tried to comfort me in private. They would take me out to lunch and drinks, as if that was their cowardly way of trying to make themselves feel better. But there was one white woman, Mariana, who worked in a department off-site, and she was someone I could talk to. She would give me advice because she wasn't so close to the situation. And, most importantly, I trusted her. She didn't look like I did, and we came from different backgrounds, but she understood and empathized with racial inequality. She served as a champion for me and helped me not feel completely isolated. Let me tell you, the support of a champion helps when you are hovering in the danger zone. Additionally, the only way that my relationship grew with my champion was because I was honest with her. People might not know how to help you if you don't tell them. When Kerry was boxing me out of some of our work projects, Mariana was able to bring me onto some of her projects. She helped make work more bearable for me in the ways she could. It wasn't her responsibility, but she was invested in my success. We all need a champion who can be our success partner.

While we are talking about workplace champions, I believe it's important to dig a little deeper. When I searched Google for the word "champion," one of the first things that came up was an "advocate" or "defender." We need to build relationships with people inside the workplace so we can identify who that champion might be for us. When I first met my champion, I had no clue she would end up being that for me one day. But I did get to know her through work, and our relationship grew. When I felt I could trust her, I shared some of the workplace issues I was experiencing, and she started to see some of them transpire for herself.

Now, my champion didn't exactly corner Kerry at an all-staff meeting and say, "I heard you were bullying Minda. You better stop it right now." Being a defender or advocate won't always look that way. She showed up for me by helping defuse the tension and creating space on projects for me that didn't require me to work directly with Kerry. She used her privilege and shifted her allyship into action. Sometimes potential champions feel like they are required to climb to the top of Mount Everest, and that scares them away from doing anything to dismantle racism. They often don't see the day-to-day, and sometimes it's the small things that make the most impact. Often, as women of color we are afraid to have critical conversations around race, because we know those types of conversations hardly ever end well. But what if we had a champion or a few champions at work who could help defuse the fear we have and help dismantle these toxic workplace environments? Let's learn how to normalize championing and advocating for racial equality in the workplace, because when more workplaces operate free of any oppression it results in a place where all people want to work and grow.

Having a healing advisor and a champion helped me better understand my tolerance-versus-threshold needs. Having a high tolerance for trauma isn't good, and we need to be aware of that as well. There are days when you can tolerate certain behaviors and other days when you know you have reached your threshold and something has to give. What will you do when either situation occurs? What tools will you use to maintain your healing? And who will you reach out to when you need someone?

I don't want you on the workplace battlefield not fully armored up. Because when your healing advisor can't get to the phone or your therapist goes on vacation, you are going to need your tools to be your own best healing advisor and champion. You might have ninety-nine work problems, but not having a healing support system won't be one of them.

YOU GOT THIS

One last thing: incorporating maintenance strategies will be important on your continued path toward healing. Even when you think you might have ascended to the mountain-top of healing, you will always have to demand respect and dignity. There will be people you come across who have no respect for justice. As Dr. Martin Luther King Jr. stated, this is about "equality over acceptance." It's not enough for business leaders to say they care about equality; they need to acknowledge racial workplace trauma as real, set up systems and trainings to prevent it, and then help employees heal from it. This should be part of the fabric of all companies, not just on the walls and in the halls, and not just on the lips of an organization's leaders but in their actions. We aren't waiting for freedom to ring—we are taking it. And freedom starts with us. Freedom has to start with our emotional and mental well-being. I hope you will consider using the tools in the chapter, and please don't be afraid to add more as you need them.

Time to Unpack and Reassess

1. How important do you think maintenance will be for you on your healing journey?
2. What are some of your racialized triggers?
3. What are some affirmations that you could use whenever you find yourself in the danger zone?
4. Who could serve as your healing advisor?
5. Who could serve as your champion in the workplace?
6. How could your relationship with your champion be most beneficial to you?
7. What would freedom in the workplace look like for you?

Chapter 7

HEALING WHILE IN HELL

Y'all gon' make me lose my mind
Up in here, up in here
—DMX, "Party Up (Up in Here)"

I can't think of too many things that suck more than working in a toxic environment. And it can be equally frustrating when you don't know when you will be able to exit stage left. You've probably been searching on all the popular job boards and updating your LinkedIn profile weekly while hoping and praying your time will come soon. You are not alone. I know that feeling all too well. You are probably asking yourself right now, *How can I heal when I'm still in hell?* I won't lie to you and tell you it's easy, but I will encourage you and give you tips on how to make work work for you while you attempt to pack lighter in a space that seems heavier than a ton of bricks.

PAIN POINTS

While I was writing this book, I was reminded of the many toxic workplaces I've had the pleasure of making work. Pretty much every job I've ever had had some underlying racist culture. Let me put it this way. You know when you go to the doctor and they ask you what level your pain is at? The doctor then asks you to rate your pain on a scale from one to ten, ten being excruciating and one barely any pain. Make no mistake, even if your pain level is at one or two, it's still uncomfortable. I started to get used to toxic workplaces, and I would create this narrative that some places weren't as painful as the last place—because this workplace was at a three, and my former job was off the scales at a fifteen. The point I want to make is, toxic is toxic and pain is pain. And twos and threes add up to a helluva lot of baggage later down your career road.

In this chapter, we are going to dig into a few critical areas to help you become right within and pack light while you wait for your next best thing. What I don't want you to do is believe that you can't find career happiness in your current state. Like I've said before, healing takes work. It takes work even if your situation seems like it might stay the same for a little longer. Because the reality is, many of us may not be able to leave right now or next year. Everyone's situation is different, and your reasons for staying are your own. I stayed at an employer for too many years because I needed the money and I wasn't finding anything comparable at that time. Yet that doesn't mean you can't find some joy in the eye of the storm. I learned to make work work for me while I was there. We will discuss what that looked like for me later in the chapter.

Also, if you're anything like I was, you don't even know what the warning signs are for a toxic work environment. I thought certain things weren't right but still normal. "Normal" meaning, as a Black woman, this is as good as it gets for us. I had nothing else to compare my experience to at that time in my career. But don't worry, we are going to discuss how to see the flashing lights sooner and find ways to navigate through some of the trauma.

I have to be honest with you. I don't have all of the answers, but I have a lot of experiences that I hope you will find helpful along your healing journey. I am going to tell you a story of an extremely toxic work environment I experienced early in my career. Let's pretend I'm a Stanford business school professor and I am presenting you with a case study on my former employer. Together we will dissect the case study and work through ways I should have handled it, knowing what I know now. Feel free to jot down notes as we work through the scenario; I am sure something might inspire you in your own situation.

A NICE PAYCHECK

Let's begin. Early in my career I was in a junior administrative role in a large corporate company. It wasn't the job I envisioned having, but it's the one that I found that paid well enough for me to have my lovely city apartment with a nice view. I originally got hired through a temp agency, and at the end of ninety days, if this company liked my work, they would offer me a permanent position. So during those ninety days I felt like I was walking on eggshells. The one thing I noticed on my first day was that all the newly hired administrative staff were women of color. At the time, I didn't think

anything of it. This was early in my career and I wasn't thinking about too much other than when I would get my next
paycheck. Oh, and doing a good job so that I would become
a permanent hire.

My first manager was someone I'll call Tiffany. I hardly
ever saw her because she delegated the managing to another
administrative staff member I'll call Nancy. Both of these
women were white. Nancy trained me and would bark orders that she claimed came down from Tiffany. Nobody liked
Nancy. I mean nobody. What I figured out was that Nancy
was acting as my supervisor even though she wasn't, and that
this lady had no shame but lots of clout. I was smart enough
to catch on that even though Tiffany was my real boss, Nancy
had the power to cut me after ninety days or recommend to
Tiffany to keep me on. Nancy was a stickler for attention to
detail, so I worked my butt off to make sure that my tasks
were executed with style and grace.

I knew that I needed to stay on Nancy's good side, even
though she was a mess for many reasons. One, she hated
where we worked, even though she had the most influence
out of all the admins. Two, she was a miserable person and
tried her best to make us miserable by always reminding us
that we were not permanent employees. She would refer to
us as "the temps." (That probably should have been my first
warning sign, but I digress.) Three, Nancy was always com-
plaining about how she hadn't received a promotion in title or money but in function. She was a little ruthless; many
of the admins that started with me didn't make it to their
ninety-day mark. Not because they couldn't file or provide a
high level of service to our internal stakeholders, but because

Nancy didn't like them as much. As women, we know all too well about the likeability trap (there's a whole book written about this by my friend Alicia Menendez). I was one of the lucky temps who was hired on permanently. Additionally, Nancy got a promotion to oversee and train all the new admins at another location. This promotion for Nancy meant that she could bring help if she needed it. So I was transferred to that location as well. I didn't necessarily want to keep working with Nancy, but the new office had a better commute, so, what the hell.

DON'T YOU KNOW THAT YOU'RE TOXIC?

There were so many toxic things happening in this environment that I don't even have the time to tell you them all. But let me fast-forward a bit for the sake of time. Nancy was the new supervisor at this location. I was the only administrative staffer who came with her from the previous location. I am not sure how I became Nancy's go-to, but for better or worse I was that person. She didn't treat me any kinder; she just knew she could trust I would get sh*t done. Soon enough, she decided to have a few temporary admins start working with us. They came over from various temp agencies around the city. All of them just so happened to be people of color. Yes, you got it right: all the admins initially were people of color, with Nancy our white boss. Her management style came with her to the new location. She would remind the admins that they were temps and at any moment they could be gone. Some didn't even make it through the first day. It was like a revolving door of admins. Of course, I would then go behind her and remind them that I became a permanent employee and that there was hope. If I knew what I know now, I would have told them to run for the hills.

Shortly after, Nancy was promoted, which meant I still reported to her and I also had to train all the new admins. If Nancy wasn't happy with their work, she would call my desk and summon me to her floor. I hated those calls because they were never good. Nancy became more and more power hungry, and whenever she knew she had crossed the line she would make some excuse. When she would call me to her office, she would tell me to go tell so-and-so to pack up their stuff and go home. I remember telling her I didn't feel comfortable doing that and perhaps this information should come from her since she was their supervisor. Then she would threaten that I would have to pack my bags too. So I would have to tell admins who I had trained and befriended that we no longer needed their services. I also served as the person who would sign their timesheets so they could get paid. I don't remember those orders being in my job description.

I started to notice a pattern with Nancy. She would call me to send people home right before their ninety-day mark. Like, where the hell was HR when you needed them? This was wrong for all sorts of reasons. There were only a few temps who made it to the other side and joined me in the permanent heavens. Truth be told, we only made it day-to-day because we had each other to hold us up. This is the part of the story where I give you my first piece of advice: if you can, try to make a work friend or two. Those people will help you push through on the days when you want to throw your hands up and run out the door screaming. We had each other to ease the pain. We had each other when Nancy would do or say something that should have resulted in her packing up her bags and leaving. We helped each other laugh when we wanted to throw a stapler across the room. I don't care what anyone says; it helps not being in isolation.

WATCHING THE CLOCK

Now, I have seen eighties movies like *Working Girl*, *Trading Places*, and *Baby Boom*, but I was not prepared as a twenty-something to deal with the Nancys of the working world and their shenanigans. I had seen my coworkers get fired in front of me, and I felt like I had no agency. There was little to no room to speak up about the inequalities. We were all oppressed. At one point, the admins all used to be able to go to lunch together. Then Nancy realized that we might be planning a coup and swapped our schedules so we couldn't take lunch at the same time. Before our final lunch together and the big band break-up, we all vowed to start looking for new jobs. This place had everyone's pain level at ten. We began to help each other with our résumés and strategizing on how to get the hell out of Nancy's regime.

The good news was that eventually everyone started to secure interviews and eventually found new jobs. The bad news was I was the only one who hadn't yet found my way out. I was so happy for my colleagues that they wouldn't have to be subjected to Nancy's ways anymore, and I was borderline depressed because I wasn't sure how or if I would find another job. I was pretty hopeless. Have you ever felt this way?

I was sad on my way to work and when I got to work. The only time I felt some relief was when I was on my way home. Even though I was all by myself (singing in my Celine Dion voice), having the support of people who understood what I was going through really helped. Sometimes it can be hard to talk to people about our workplace trauma when they can't relate to the experience or you think it's happening to only you. Having a support system can be part of the healing process. One of those temps who made it to the other side became like a big sister to me. Years after working for Nancy, we would always have a good laugh about our old boss and those early days. It served as a twisted source of joy. Sometimes time has to pass before you can see your pain in that way.

While I waited for my change to come, I had to find a productive way to handle and process my current distress. If you are currently dealing with a similar situation, here are three actions that helped me heal while I still had to endure that workplace:

1. **Center Your Goals.** I wasn't officially a supervisor, but I sure did have some of those responsibilities. I started to ask Nancy for additional supervisory duties (the ones that weren't a direct violation of somebody's HR handbook), such as learning the budget, ordering supplies, and working with some of the senior leaders to support their teams more effectively. Remember when I said make work work for you? I used that hellhole to build out my résumé, so as I was shopping for a new job, I could tell my career story in a more robust

way. Perhaps making work work for you might be using a professional-development stipend and getting a certification to help you land your next role. The bottom line is that you can try to get what you need while you're still there. Learning to center yourself is part of that healing process, especially when you are currently in a place that is a source of trauma.

2. **Mental Health Days.** I had racked up quite a few sick and vacation days. Since I was sick of that place, one day a month I would take what I call a mental health day. I would have one day off during the month that was mine. I might visit my parents or call up one of my friends and meet up for lunch. I knew that I needed a break from that place outside of the regular Saturday and Sunday. That one extra day a month helped me get my life together and helped me feel like I had a little control. It's actually a practice I took with me to other jobs as well. Let me tell you, there is nothing like a good mental health day, so take one if you need to.

3. **Set Boundaries.** I didn't have the best luck with boundary setting when I was in my first corporate job. In what ways do you think I missed the mark creating boundaries with Nancy? It's easier to see when someone else needs to set boundaries than when we do. I hope you won't make some of the same mistakes I made with Nancy. Draw your line in the sand with colleagues early on, even if they hold a higher title.

Because I was the youngest and feared losing my job, I thought that I couldn't set boundaries. But no matter how hard things might get, we can always set them. That is the part of the equation we can solve. We can't force anyone to do what we want or hear us out, but we can say what needs to be said. It wasn't until all of my work friends left that I finally gave myself permission to set some healthy boundaries with Nancy. I no longer gave out pink slips and I didn't work overtime while she hung out on the higher floor doing who knows what. It was extremely hard, but it helped make my time there a little more bearable. As women of color, we can't afford to let the Nancys of the working world traumatize us. The wild part about it all? None of us admins felt we had the agency to set boundaries because we were considered to be the bottom of the food chain. Perhaps if we had gone to her floor together and established at least one or two boundaries, the toxicity wouldn't have been so bad. If you are in a similar situation, please try to do what needs to be done so you can have some peace. We have been conditioned to center everyone else; it's time that we start to put our mental health first, or it will trickle down and affect our physical health too.

The good news for me is I did find my way out of that place, and I had a lot of new skills that helped me land a better job with a higher title and more managerial responsibilities. Sometimes all is not lost.

I am not going to tell you that going through any of that was easy, because it wasn't. And I am not going to BS you and tell you to put those three actions into motion, snap your fingers, and things will get better. One active ingredient in my survival was that I chose to take the control back from Nancy in my most authentic way possible. Let's take a pause right now. What would that look like for you? This is an opportunity for you to choose your own adventure. I am not saying you should burn bridges, but if the place sucks, choose the potential outcome you would like to have and take actions that center you. Take the actions that center your well-being, because clearly they are taking actions that center their toxicity. What do you have to lose? Lastly, I mentioned therapy and speaking to a spiritual advisor in previous chapters. Now might be a good time to explore which of those tools might be most impactful for your continued healing. Because you don't have to go through this alone.

FLASHING LIGHTS

In 2019, I interviewed Sarah Morgan, chief excellence officer of BuzzARooney LLC, for my podcast *Secure the Seat.* Morgan runs a management-consulting boutique based in North Carolina. We discussed the warning signs of a toxic workplace, and it is one of my most popular episodes to date. Morgan shared so many insightful gems that I wanted to pass them along to you as additional resources in your healing tool kit for the days you might need them most. She was able to offer relevant advice from her past experiences that I believe will help as you plot your next move.

The first question I asked Morgan was about her definition of a toxic workplace. She defined it as "any atmosphere where the vibe, the energy, or the people are causing a disruption to your professional productivity." She mentioned that sometimes a toxic work environment can start out subtle and later lead to more blatant occurrences. A subtle example could be low enthusiasm for the company potluck. An extreme example might be high turnover.

Later in our conversation, I asked her about some warning signs she had observed in past toxic work environments. She mentioned a culture of low enthusiasm, low productivity, high turnover, and leadership disengagement. Morgan said it might be hard to rally people in the break room or virtual conference room to celebrate colleagues' birthdays or attend after-hours activities, because many employees were experiencing low morale. It's easy to see when hardly anyone is happy at work.

She felt it was equally important to mention some of the behaviors women of color should be aware of to help prevent us from falling into a spiral of negativity and compounded trauma. If you find yourself being less present and not giving a darn, this might mean you have completely tapped out and that you're only doing the bare minimum at work. Also, if you find yourself constantly venting or gossiping with other colleagues about your discontentment, you might be in the sunken place. We aren't saying you don't have the right to feel this way, but misery loves company and, as Morgan said, "nothing good will come of it." I agree.

At the end of my interview with Morgan, I asked her how women of color can turn some of those behaviors around. Because the part of the equation we can solve is how we handle it. She gave four tangible examples that I think you will find useful, and you might even want to add to this list.

1. Only talk with people who will help you stay accountable. Meaning, if there are colleagues who you only

talk to when discussing all the people who drive y'all crazy, start to shift the conversation to help each other find solutions to these problems. Shifting the dynamics of the conversation will help you keep your integrity intact. Also, Morgan made a great point that if you need a moment to vent, set a timer and, once you've gotten it out of your system, keep it moving.

2. Start writing your letter of resignation today. This is your opportunity to set your intentions. You don't have to get ready if you stay ready. Even though you might not be able to hit the send button on it tonight, drafting your resignation letter will help you release some of the tension.

3. Start writing your exit interview right now. If your company offers an exit interview, what questions would you love to answer? This is another opportunity to find some healing. You might not have anyone in leadership who will hear you out because your environment is way too toxic. But that shouldn't stop you from getting closer to your healing. Shout, and let it all out!

4. Cultivate other areas of your life. When Morgan was experiencing an unbearable working environment, she started blogging, and that helped her channel that pent-up energy into other outlets. Her blog later turned into her HR-consulting business. This is also what helped me back in 2015. I was leaving a toxic workplace and I decided I needed to write to get some things off my chest. My Monday career newsletter later turned into a company, a podcast, and a bestselling book. Having other outlets can be a form of healing.

These are just some practices you can incorporate to help you thrive in an environment that is trying to oppress you. Please make the decision today to turn that oppression into power that only you can harness.

WHAT ELSE?

I know it's hard not to feel a sense of rage or sadness every day when you walk into your office. Trust me, I get it. You might even feel like you don't have any fight left, but before we move on, I want to share one more piece of advice for you to consider. Don't forget that you have choices. You can also choose to hold your company accountable legally. I can only imagine what might have popped into your head when you read or heard me say it. You read that line correctly, and we don't talk enough about taking our complaints of racial discrimination to our human resources department or the Equal Employment Opportunity Commission.

For some context, a recent *Vox* piece reported that while Black workers make up 13 percent of the US workforce, they file 26 percent of racial-discrimination claims to the EEOC and their partner agencies. Racial discrimination is still taking place in the country, and under Title VII of the Civil Rights Act of 1964, it's illegal to harass any person at work because of their race or color. This includes verbal, written, nonverbal, or visual racial harassment in the workplace. If you are currently experiencing racial discrimination or trauma in the workplace, please document everything. There is nothing too small or too big to document. Even if you never use your documentation to file a claim, you will still have a paper trail of your experiences, when or if you decide to use them.

To be clear, I am not a legal professional, but I want you to know all of your options when you are still in a racialized environment. Healing for you might result in going to the HR liaison and making them aware of what you've been experiencing. If you are considering this as an option, you might also tell someone at work you trust, so that you have documentation of telling someone who works with you. Many of us rarely report our racialized experiences because retaliation might come with it or we don't have any extra energy left to fight such a huge battle. I am not telling you one way is better than the other, but if you want to explore legal action, I suggest seeking legal advice and taking a look at the EEOC website to explore the steps you can take to submit a claim. Just remember that the system was created to silence our voices. Only you can decide what's best for you.

BEWARE OF PTSD

According to the National Center for PTSD, there is something that some military veterans experience called a "moral injury." A moral injury is defined as "a construct that describes extreme and unprecedented life experiences including harmful aftermath of exposure to such events." I don't know about you, but I've experienced some racial discrimination that I would deem as harmful events. Not only that, but the exposure to those extreme experiences did not help me in some of my future work environments, because I was still suffering from their aftermath. Those experiences created baggage that I carried from one job to the next. The trippy thing about it is, even if my current employer didn't have the same bad characters as my last, I was susceptible to the triggers from previous exposure to racial assaults. Racial trauma is extremely daunting. It's a burden we shouldn't have to carry, because we didn't cause the pain. If you are experiencing fear, anxiety, shame, and low self-esteem, these might be some of the signs of PTSD. Don't be afraid to reach out to a healer who can help you process your pain. During this time, you can still find a way to build your resilience. And, I can't stress it enough, you don't have to go through your healing journey alone.

In 2020, the world was experiencing a health crisis known as COVID-19. Dr. Bernice King, the daughter of Dr. Martin Luther King Jr. and Mrs. Coretta Scott King, tweeted, "It is traumatizing to be living through a global pandemic and living through the viciousness of racism at the same time." There are triggers that people of color will experience in this country from the office to the doctor to the streets. For those business leaders who want to use their influence for good, I would suggest helping implement on-site wellness programs for people of color, to assist in healing from the systemic racism embedded in company culture. This might include on-site professional coaching, therapy, and group workshops. I also think we can collectively start to hold our leaders and managers accountable for being complicit in toxic behavior. People of color shouldn't have to be subjected to racism, offer solutions on how to deal with it, and heal at the same time.

It's not enough for companies to commit to the popularity of anti-racism training. We also have to address racial justice practices. Racial justice is defined by the National Education Association as "the systematic fair treatment of people of all races, resulting in equitable opportunities and outcomes for all." In my opinion, racial justice for Black women and all women of color is investing in tools that dismantle systemic oppression in the workplace. That shouldn't just include pay transparency but mental health services as well.

EVERYDAY ACTIONS

The last area I want to focus on is toxic people in the workplace. Sometimes I hear people say, "XYZ company is racist." I would push back on that to say, *There are some people at XYZ company who are racist, and the leadership at that company is encouraging a harmful environment at work. Both parties are equally at fault for the culture of the company or organization.*

I wish there was an island where we could drop off all the bad characters and let karma have their way with them for all the racialized oppression they've caused us. But since we can't, let's discuss some tangible ways to help you right now. Let's rechannel the trauma and energy that's causing you pain while you're still working for your current employer. I created the Affirmation Pyramid to help you center yourself on the days you feel triggered or exposed to racism. I can't come to work with you and check everyone when they are being out of pocket (because I would if I could), yet I want you to feel like I am there in spirit.

AFFIRMATIONS FOR YOURSELF

The Affirmation Pyramid is broken down into five sections: *pause*, *acknowledge*, *document*, *redistribute*, and *affirm*. Pause is at the bottom, as the first step, and as you take the next steps you rise up the pyramid and arrive at the top, at affirm. Every time you use the pyramid, I want you to make sure you end with an affirmation. You might not be working in an affirming environment, but like the gospel singer Donald Lawrence told us, "sometimes you have to encourage yourself." Let me walk you through how you can use the Affirmation Pyramid. I also want to point out that you might find you want to use the Affirmation Pyramid in other ways that work better for you down the line, or you can create your own. Think of this as another tool in your healing tool kit.

For example, say Janine is a Puerto Rican woman who has been dealing with her toxic manager, Bobby. Currently, Bobby's team is working remotely, and Janine is happy because it cuts down on the racial trauma she experiences while in the office with Bobby. Bobby is always referring to Janine as "spicy" and sometimes even calls her J.Lo in meetings instead of her name. Janine has had conversations with Bobby, but they went nowhere. He just told her she takes things too seriously. During their weekly team meeting via their company's virtual conference platform, Bobby hollers out on the call: "Cinco de Mayo is coming up. Janine, you're Mexican— we will let you plan it." Bobby quickly ends the meeting and Janine is sitting on her couch, furious. One added detail: Janine has been trying to transfer to another team, but it probably won't happen for another six months. She is not in a position to up and quit, although she thinks about it five times a day.

If I were Janine, this is how I would use the Affirmation Pyramid:

1. **Pause.** It's important to take a beat and breathe. Our impulses might have us writing a scathing email to Bobby, or on the verge of quitting or getting fired. If possible, inhale through your nose and breathe out through your mouth three to five times. We want to make sure you release the negativity and center yourself.

2. **Acknowledge.** Name the racialized trauma Bobby has again subjected you to. You are tired of telling yourself he doesn't mean any harm when that narrative is not true. Acknowledge his actions, then acknowledge how they made you feel. Let's shift the focus to your feelings. As women of color, we often push our feelings aside, not giving ourselves permission to feel the emotions, but you also don't have to stay in them for long.

3. **Document.** Write down what happened and any pertinent information around the racialized experience within your team meeting.

4. **Redistribute.** Right now, you might be feeling blindsided, confused, hurt, or angry. You have every right to feel everything that you are feeling at this moment or might feel later in the day. It's time for you to take your feelings and redistribute them in ways that benefit you. This might mean journaling about the experience, going to HR, having a conversation with Bobby, or helping start a speaker series on racism in the workplace

through your employee resource group. The point I want to make here is to rechannel that negative energy away from Bobby and take the power back.

5. **Affirm.** Clearly Bobby is racist, sexist, and probably some other -ists we could fill in the blank with. But this moment in time ain't got sh*t to do with Bobby and everything should be centered around you. You might need to say a prayer, read your favorite poem, or pull up that Audre Lorde quote that makes you want to turn into Nefertiti. The most important part of affirming yourself is knowing that this situation isn't your fault, so please don't let your mind hit you with any internalized guilt. Remind yourself that you are more than enough. This time in your life is only part of your story. There is healing and redemption on the other side of this mountain.

It's important to mention, you don't have to race through the pyramid; there is no time limit for each step. One person might use it in the morning and affirm themselves fifteen minutes later at the top of the pyramid, and another person might need all week to make it to the middle. As I said before, there isn't one way to heal. You get to determine how to use this tool. And you also get to decide if this tool could work for you.

Sometimes we just need something in the moment to help stop the bleeding when we have been racially assaulted. I hope the Affirmation Pyramid can serve as a source of strength, resilience, and hope when you need it most.

TORN IN-BETWEEN THE TWO

Some of you might be at a crossroads right now, meaning you don't know if you should stay at this job or leave. You might feel like every day is a struggle to wake up and work with those ignorant people or deal with that obnoxious manager. You don't know what you might do if someone says one more racist thing to you. You are already on the edge. If you are honest with yourself, you probably would have left already if you could. I know that feeling, and it's painful. But do you remember that song "Torn" by LeToya Luckett? I was thinking about it in regard to some of the hard questions we must ask ourselves to get the answers we need. Because, as much advice as I have given in this book, this is a decision you have to make on your own. The line in the song that really resonated with me is: "A part of me wants to say goodbye / A part of me is asking why." Are these not the thoughts that swirl through our heads when we are contemplating what our next step should be? We legit feel torn, right?

When I was in the situation with Nancy, as much as I wanted to quit, I had responsibilities and I had to wait until I was in a position to leave for a better opportunity. If I should stay or go was an easy decision for me to make. I definitely needed to find a better environment, because the toxicity was bad for my health. There wasn't a day that went by where I wasn't searching on Monster.com or Hotjobs or one of those other early 2000s job sites. I think I even asked Jeeves to help me at some point. There were times I felt really desperate for a new job because I wanted out so bad. Yet I was not in a position to just get on the elevator, hit level one, drive home, and never return. Maybe your situation is similar. Or maybe you haven't even tried looking for a new job out of fear. I've heard many women make the comment that they would rather stay with the devil they know. In theory I get that, but all devils make your life feel like hell, even if they are the ones you know. If you are already in a traumatized state of existence, I hope you won't rationalize bad behavior. If fear is holding you back from trying to strategize your escape route, let's talk about some ways you might be able to mitigate that fear. Because the last thing you need during your healing process is to deal with trauma while being scared to be great and have better.

These toxic work environments tend to have us questioning after a while if we can even do better somewhere else. We are in such a bad work relationship that we might think this job is as good as it gets. As with any abusive relationship, it's always hard to leave. I won't pretend to know your situation. You might have a savings account you can live on for the next six months to a year and decide your sanity means more and quit tomorrow. Or you might be in a situation like a woman I met named Terrie. Terrie was working in a racially toxic environment in higher education. Her youngest son was a senior in high school. Part of Terrie's benefit package was that her children would have 80 percent of their college tuition paid for, as long as she was working full-time for her employer. She had already put three of her children through college, and she just needed to push through to get the youngest his cap and gown. Her sacrifice was worth it to her. She said that when the last one makes it across the college graduation stage, she will be out of there so fast they will think she was a track-and-field star. Remember when I said we have to find ways to make work work for us. Terrie was looking for ways to heal through the trauma to get to her desired state. She didn't want to give her manager the pleasure of pushing her out before she got what she needed for her family. And every day, Terrie reminded herself of her why, and that helped reset the table for her each and every morning. Yet Terrie was very candid that if she didn't have the benefit of college tuition, she would have left a long time ago. There was no other benefit to staying in that environment.

Another woman that I spoke to, Bonita, was very honest that she was afraid to leave, for two reasons: (1) she feared leaving her current employer because she didn't want to end up in another toxic workplace, and (2) she feared not being able to find a good job because she was over forty. As much as Bonita knew she deserved an environment she could thrive in and not just survive, all of her fears had her feeling stuck. Many of us know that fear is really good at keeping us where we are. Let's be honest, starting over, no matter how old you are, can be scary.

When I left my very stable nine-to-five job to grow my own business, I was terrified. I am the type of person who needs stability. I worried if I would be able to make as much money as I used to make. I worried about the great health insurance I had and what I would have to switch over to. There were so many unknowns that created more fear than I knew what to do with. But my curiosity was larger than my fear. I knew that I could not go another year in the environment I was working at. I refused to let that employer take some of the best years of my life and mental health. But only I could make that decision for myself. For a year or more, I started saving money just in case my business wasn't able to turn a profit. I couldn't predict the future, but I knew I could at least keep myself afloat for a year, and truth be told I needed a break from that place to continue on with my healing. Thankfully, as I write this to you, by the grace of God, I have been working for myself since I left that employer. I don't know what the future holds, but it was the best decision I have ever made for myself. Those fears come and go at times, but I think that is also part of my PTSD.

I believe that being apprehensive and strategic is important with any decision you make about your financial well-being. Feeling concerned about what the outcomes might be on the other side is normal. As I assessed my next steps, I wanted to share with you a few things I did as I prepared for my big escape.

First, talk to other people. I started to go to networking events and joined listservs with other people who left their day job to start their own business. I wanted to consume as much information as I could. I wanted to learn some of the pitfalls and resources to help make my transition smoother. Another example: Let's say you want to work for a specific company. You could reach out to other women of color who currently work there or used to work there and inquire about their experiences. This is a great way to address some of your concerns before you leave your job or apply for another one. Think about your current pain points and make sure you address them when you go on your listening tour. We can both agree that no place is perfect, but racial trauma is what you are trying to get away from, so ask honest questions, center your needs, and make informed decisions about your next role. Additionally, if you are on the fence about what to do, the more information you have, the better.

Second, keep your résumé updated. What if someone has a great opportunity they want to offer you, but you haven't updated your résumé in seven years? Part of our healing is preparing for our next best thing. All of the skills you've acquired and sales numbers you helped the company hit, make sure they are on your résumé or personal website. Your future employer might be looking for what you have to offer without you even applying for it. Sometimes we need to be reminded of how awesome we are as an employee. Having your résumé up-to-date is one less stressor to have on your plate. I had my résumé ready even though I was plotting to build my own company, because you just never know what might come your way. In fact, I had an opportunity to become an adjunct professor at New York University's Wagner Graduate School of Public Service. The opportunity came out of the blue and I had to send my résumé immediately. Thank God I had it ready, because I might have missed out. I always wanted to be a faculty member, but I thought that was for some time in the distant future. I mentioned that I was a little concerned financially, and having this new extra income really helped. I would never tell you to do something that I haven't tried myself.

Third, renew your mindset. When you have been living and breathing toxic colleagues and managers, that toxicity will no doubt affect how you see yourself. One scripture that my pastor gave to me when I was having a tough time trying to stay mentally healthy while still in that environment was John 10:10.

John 10:10 in the Message version of the Bible reads: "A thief is only there to steal and kill and destroy. I came so they can have real and eternal life, more and better life than they ever dreamed of." This scripture can be interpreted into your current situation. There will more than likely be things in this world that will try to steal our joy, but ultimately we possess more power, and we have full authority to take our power back and live our best lives. The thief in this context is our workplace, and if we continue using our tools and make healing a priority even when we feel opposition, we will break free from what might be trying to destroy us. Even if you aren't a religious or spiritual person, the same principles still apply if you believe you deserve better. News flash, we have colleagues who will never have to experience the racial trauma we do just because they are white, and if we don't leave some of these environments, they will keep trying to steal our joy.

If you decide to quit or stay a little longer, I want you to make sure you are doing it because you believe that this is or isn't the place for you, not because of fear. At the end of Le-Toya's song, she sings, "But something's telling me I should leave you alone." Again, I am not telling you what you should or shouldn't do, but most of the time, you know the answer. Anything worth fighting for will always take courage. And now might be the time you have to fight for yourself.

YOU GOT NEXT

Trying to navigate a racially toxic environment isn't easy, but you have a community of women rooting for you and holding space for you until you are able to enter your next best thing. But never forget the wise words of Toni Morrison: "You are your best thing." Some of these workplaces will attempt to break you down and have you carrying around these racial wounds for life, but I am here to tell you, you are not your wounds. You might feel like you're alone in that environment, but from here on out, I want you to take us with you into those rooms when you need strength. Harness our collective power when you feel like you don't have much left. You are stronger than you think, and healing is on the way. I am excited to see what tools you use in your healing tool kit to help you get through this time in your life. On the days when you feel torn, ask yourself this question: If I had a son or daughter, would I want them to experience a workplace like the one I am in? If that answer is no, then what steps are you going to take to make sure you are right within? You have the ability to find your heaven.

Time to Unpack and Reassess

1. Some of the information we covered in this chapter might have brought up some feelings for you. Write down how you are feeling and write out the themes that resonated with you.

2. If you work in a toxic environment, who are the people you need to stay clear of to help you create a safe space?

3. Is there anyone at work who you might need to create better boundaries with to sustain a healthy state of mind? If so, why?

4. Jot down three affirmations that you can use for your Affirmation Pyramid to remind you that you are your best thing.

5. What are some ways you can redistribute the trauma when you experience it at work?

Chapter 8

YOU ARE NOT ALONE

We are family
I got all my sisters with me
—Sister Sledge, "We Are Family"

In the spring of 2019, I remember reading an open letter in *Variety* by a former executive at CBS, Whitney Davis. In the article, Davis shared that, according to her personal experience, CBS had a culture of racial discrimination, sexual harassment, and systemic racism. She called the network out on its "white problem." It was the first time I had read a claim like this from a high-profile Black woman executive. As I read the article, I was able to put myself in Davis's shoes. She was a Black woman speaking her truth about a major network. Now, I wasn't working for a major network, but I did know how it felt to speak my truth out loud. I could only imagine how much courage it took for her to tell her story and walk away from her decade-and-a-half career at CBS. I found the article so refreshing because she allowed herself to be vulnerable, and often Black women can't do that in the workplace without some blowback. She went on to share her racialized trauma by describing it in this way: "I took medical leave for what I initially thought was anxiety and stress from postpartum depression. I've since learned that the source of my anxiety and stress was CBS' toxic work environment." She also described how her therapist and attorney advised her to negotiate an exit package. I mention Davis's story because there has to be a place for women of color to share our trauma, not just for the sake of acknowledging it, but to let other women of color know they are not alone. We don't have to accept workplace discrimination, and hearing these stories lets the rest of us know that women who look like us have fought systemic racism at the highest levels, which is helpful when you are considering if you should do the same.

REPRESENTATION WILL ALWAYS MATTER

If we don't have representation and hear our stories told, we are likely to believe three things: (1) Racism is an isolated situation. (2) If we do experience a racialized workplace, we should just shut up and make it work. And (3) there are no Black women taking these corporate giants to court. I am thankful for women like Whitney Davis who are sharing their stories on a larger stage, otherwise we wouldn't know we could do it too. Please know that you are not alone. In this chapter, I will highlight women like Davis who have been in your shoes, who are healing through the trauma, and who are fighting like hell to make the workplace better than they found it. Let us take a moment of silence for all the women of color who took some of these companies and organizations to task for the inhumane, racialized treatment they experienced. Some fought in the court system for years and walked away with only their word, while others won their discrimination lawsuits. And there are others who chose to hold their leaders accountable and stay in their position. We need all types of women, in various spaces, fighting this equity battle.

The other thing I want to be clear on is that I am not advising you to sue your employer. Even at the height of some really awful experiences, I never took legal action. But what I am saying is that knowing that you are not alone and knowing your options can help you make an informed decision about what you will accept, fight for, or leave behind. There is no right or wrong way to do it, but every decision you make to center yourself will take courage, because healing takes courage. I imagine that some of the women who read Davis's story in 2019 channeled her courage and energy and were able to tell their stories in 2020, about their experiences at companies like Away, Glossier, Pinterest, and many others. Self-love will sometimes require us to be radically different. Meaning, when Black women share their racialized stories, or any story for that matter, we are defying the status quo. Our stories are not centered in US history or policy, and as we share and heal we collectively amplify our own stories. Because, as the cofounder of the Nomadic Archivists Project Miranda Mims says, "We are the memory workers." It's up to us to tell our own stories and preserve them.

IT HIT HOME

There are many stories like Whitney Davis's and mine, but not all of our stories receive a platform, so we have to provide one for ourselves. Yet another story that I found compelling was reported by the *New York Times* podcast *The Daily*. It was about a young Black woman named Julia Bond, an assistant apparel designer at Adidas. During the George Floyd protests in summer 2020, she called out Adidas on its treatment and lack of representation for Black employees and other marginalized groups at the most senior levels of the company—inequities she had noticed taking place. Bond used her lunch hour to protest Adidas while she continued to work there. As I was listening to her tell her story, I thought about how badass it is to call your company out, advocate for yourself and your colleagues, and still do your job—that is exactly what I mean by being radically different. Bond saw Adidas making external claims that Black Lives Matter, but as a Black woman she didn't feel the same love on the inside. She challenged Adidas in quite a revolutionary way. When I heard her story, I thought of a young Angela Davis and Claudette Colvin, pushing for nothing less than equity with their Black fists up in the air.

Even though 2020 was a dumpster fire for many, something interesting started to take place after the horrific killings of George Floyd and Breonna Taylor. The volcano of racism finally erupted. And the eruption was extremely painful for many communities of color. We found ourselves in a racial reckoning, resulting in a national conversation about racial tension in the United States in a way I had never experienced before. For example, six months before the global health pandemic known as COVID-19, I was still promoting my first book, *The Memo*. At that time, not a lot of companies were comfortable talking about microaggressions and racism, which created some reluctance to have me as a speaker. Some companies feared that having me come in and speak would open up Pandora's racism-does-exist-here box, and they weren't ready to show me behind the scenes. Fast-forward to 2020, and within three weeks of the racial eruption I had so many speaking engagements to discuss how the workplace can invest in women of color and dismantle racism that I had to turn work down or pass other names along because I couldn't meet the demand.

During the pandemic, I guess you could say I was booked and busy. Yet it was the most bittersweet moment of my life. On the one hand, I found the shift—that white people finally wanted to have hard conversations around race—encouraging. On the other hand, as a Black woman I found it hard to grieve the racial trauma and reckoning I was experiencing while educating others on racism and how it has killed careers for women who look like me. This moment in history sparked courage in so many Black women, who took their voices to the social media streets and spoke their truth about the inequality they were facing in the workplace. Some of these career revolutionaries were calling out their companies for praising Black Lives Matter publicly while needing to have a reckoning internally. Black and Brown women were using social media not just to retweet a meme or two, but to spill the tea and call out past employers that had forced them out of the careers they had worked so hard to secure.

As they started to tell their stories, the floodgates began to break. It was a bonfire of bad experiences due to racial trauma setting the internet ablaze. It wasn't just Me Too; it was yes, me too, and let me tell you all about it. I remember reading some of those stories and tweets like *Yasss! Speak your truth.* And to be very clear, I wasn't relishing in someone else's pain, but I knew as these women were sharing their stories, they were finding their healing as well. When I shared some of my workplace broken-heart stories in *The Memo*, I didn't realize how therapeutic it would be. It allowed me to start peeling away the layers around my trauma and get to the heart of the matter, which was racism. Another aspect that I didn't realize would happen when I told my story was that it would resonate with other women. My story was their story. And as I spoke about some of the issues and challenges that I faced in the workplace, other women were nodding, because they were able to see their career narratives reflected back at them. From city to city while on book tour, we were able to have a collective healing session. During our two hours together, there would be laughs, tears, and hugs. There is something about sharing your truth and knowing that you aren't alone.

RACISM KILLS CAREERS

When we find the strength to share our stories in a journal, on a blog, or to a friend or family member, we are breaking down our trauma bit by bit. I firmly believe we were not created to carry our trauma alone. We've gotten good at holding it and hiding it, yet that trauma was never supposed to happen, therefore we shouldn't have to be the ones to carry it around. The workplace trauma that many of us have experienced has killed our careers. I spoke to over two hundred women of color while writing this book and asked them about their experiences in the workplace—women who worked in law, education, retail, medicine, and corporate America. When they spoke of their workplace trauma, there was one common theme: racism killed their original and hard-built careers. Many have learned to pivot, but it doesn't mean they don't still mourn their past professional lives.

One woman painfully recounted a story of working for her employer for almost fifteen years, only to show up one morning and discover that her keycard no longer worked. She found out she was fired from the company's security guard. She had started speaking out about holding the company accountable for its racial inequities, and within months her entire world was shaken. It was stories like hers, others', and my own that made me realize how we had to mourn the careers we once had. I remember the year racism killed my career, while others mourn dates of 1979, 1988, 1994, 2018, and on and on. To be clear, racism isn't a person; it's a system of people who uphold white supremacy. Even though racism killed our first careers and some second careers, many of us knew that healing was on the other side. If we started to share our stories with other women who looked like us, then they might be able to heal too. But most importantly, they would know they weren't alone. You might be thinking, *Yeah, racism killed my career too*, and I am sorry that you had to experience that. But I am hopeful that you will find the tools to heal from the pain. I bet if many of us had known each other prior to our RIP-career dates, we could have helped each other in more ways than one. But unfortunately many of us are battling these systems of oppression in isolation. The good news is that we don't have to fight these systems alone any longer.

CHANGE YOUR MIND

One of my favorite sermons I like to listen to on repeat is "Radical Expectations" by Sarah Jakes Roberts. Every time I listen to it, I gain a new understanding of God's expectations of me as I walk through my healing journey. Recently what stood out to me was the line: "Change your expectations of this moment." Roberts went on to say that, yes, you might have experienced trauma, but it doesn't mean that you have to expect trauma in your new experience. Of course when she said it, I immediately thought of the workplace. Just because we have experienced racialized trauma at work doesn't mean that we have to expect racialized trauma at every employer after. We can change the expectations of our work environment at any time.

It's really profound when you think about it. Part of not being alone is holding others accountable, if we choose, for our pain. We can have so much power over our trauma if we have faith and activate our voices. Later in her sermon, Roberts says, "That pain will turn into purpose. . . . I thought that [pain] was going to be the end of me but turns out it was really the birthing of me, and I came out on the other side a different version of me." Straight up bars! She was spitting that fire! When we allow healing to take place, we have the ability to create and experience a new version of ourselves. Remember when Bishop Vashti McKenzie said that we don't want to go back to who we were, but we want to get closer to being whole. Just like a butterfly goes through a metamorphosis, healing sheds our cocoon and we become a new version of ourselves.

Even though my former career died, the year after I was able to start the process of my metamorphosis. I took my trauma and turned my pain into a new story. I had to go into my cocoon and emerge as a new woman. In order to heal, I had to go through that process. And in this chapter, you will find other women who went through their process too. You might remember the exact date of your career death, but you will also remember the year you rose again.

FRAN'S IN CHARGE

Fran Parham had a very successful career as a human resources executive at a Fortune 500 company. When I spoke with Parham, she told me her ten-year anniversary was coming up. And the anniversary she was referring to was when her former employer destroyed a career she once loved. She would be retiring within the next couple of years if she were still there. Racism killed Parham's career in 2011. Parham is the woman I mentioned earlier—when her key card no longer worked, the security guard informed her that she was no longer employed at the company. As we dug deeper into her story, I asked Parham if she had experienced healing from her racialized trauma. She replied, "I feel like I have healed, but I have scar tissue. I have learned to compartmentalize the pain. I am always reminded of the scar every day, yet my scar fuels me to advocate for other women in the work I do now." Because Parham knew how hard her former corporate role had been as an African American woman, she started a workshop series called Sharpen Your Skills. The Sharpen Your Skills platform helps professional women and women of color position themselves with the necessary skills to advance in a working world full of unwritten rules and unspoken skill requirements.

As I continued to interview Parham, I had to ask her if she regretted taking legal action against her former employer. She said, "I grew up in a house with parents who taught me to always fight for the little man. I only mirrored what I knew to do, fight injustice." Being in an HR role, Parham knew the rules of engagement. And even though she had experienced some racial discrimination in her role, she filed her suit for the other people of color who were experiencing discrimination too. She wanted to make the workplace better than how she'd found it.

Parham recalled being in a meeting with her manager before all the crap hit the fan. He told her, "I am disappointed in you that you would put the company through such turmoil." That C-suite executive had a lot of nerve to be more concerned with "the company" than with what the talent was experiencing at the hands of people like him. Some folks love to be both the oppressor and the victim. Please pick one, Jim—you can't have it both ways!

Parham went on to fight her lawsuit for almost five years. I asked her, if she had to do it all over again, would she? She said, "What I want other women of color to know is it takes courage and there will be an emotional and financial cost.

But what kept me fighting was knowing I was helping future women of color who will be hired there." She also said, "I want other women of color to be aware that when you enter into such a high-stakes situation, be prepared for those who you used to call work friends to turn their backs on you, and the company you were once so loyal to to act like you never worked there." Parham said the betrayal of former colleagues and managers who she was once very close with was the part of the journey that hurt the most, and dealing with it took some healing as well.

As I ended my conversation with Parham, she told me about a painful experience regarding her family. During this time in her career, her father's health was declining. She chose not to share her battle against her former employer with him. So every morning she would put on her business suit and head out the door for the day as if she was still working as that HR executive. But when she left the house, she was fighting an entirely different battle. Her father had been a sharecropper, and she didn't want to do anything that would disappoint him or cause a further disruption to his health. I felt the pain Parham spoke of when it comes to making decisions as a Black woman, because so many of our families depend on us for financial or emotional support. Sometimes we don't take the stand we might want to take because so much is tied to our success. Often Black and Brown women don't get to make the choice that's best for them but must choose what's best for the entire family. They might want to quit, but how many family members' lives would that impact? It's a real situation and a burden that I don't think many of our white women counterparts have to take into consideration when they are deciding to stay or leave a company. But that is probably another part of our healing for another day and another book.

I thought about the courage it took for Parham to take legal action against a corporate giant and hold it accountable. She ended up with a small settlement, yet the dollar amount couldn't match the emotional and financial pain that occurred. As we ended the interview, Parham said, "I would do it all over again, I would put my business suit back on and fight, because I now know it was bigger than me." Fran Parham's story reminds me of author Michele Wallace and her book *Black Macho and the Myth of the Superwoman*. Wallace challenged Black women to write their own narratives, and that is exactly what Parham did. Because of her workplace courage, others will know that if they feel the need to go the distance, it's possible.

Parham was candid with me that there are times when she feels triggered, even after all these years. She feels triggered when she reads stories of other women of color or companies who make commitments to their Black employees, like her former employer did, when she knows the real truth. Her Black life didn't matter to them when she decided to activate her voice for good. Parham is not letting anything slow her advocacy down or prevent her from moving forward. Her scars are still there, but they don't hurt as much as they used to. She doesn't let those old wounds stop her purpose and passion for helping other women who find themselves in a similar situation.

MOURNING VERSUS GRIEVING

Another common theme I have found in the conversations I've had with other women of color is the mourning and grieving process related to loss of a career or job, especially one that you worked so hard to secure, only to have to leave or walk away due to racism or another form of discrimination. According to the dictionary, grief is defined as "deep or poignant distress caused by or as if by bereavement," and mourning is defined as "a period of time during which stages of grief are shown."

Some might think grief and mourning are the same, but they are more like cousins. Grief is the internal emotion we feel from a loss, and mourning is the external emotion that we might exhibit due to that loss. For example, Elisabeth Kübler-Ross identified the five stages of grief. Those stages are denial, anger, bargaining, depression, and acceptance. And there is no doubt in my mind that during our healing process we might feel each of these emotions as we grieve our career loss. As I began to study grief and the role it plays in the healing process, I found that in order to heal, the grief we are experiencing at some point might turn into mourning.

William Worden added on to Kübler-Ross's work and asked us to consider the four tasks of mourning to help us get to our finish line. Those four tasks are: to accept the reality of the loss, to process the pain of grief, to adjust to a world without the deceased, and to find an enduring connection with the deceased in the midst of embarking on a new life. Worden's tasks of mourning primarily refer to the loss of a loved one, but I think we can use them while mourning the loss of our career too.

I appreciate that we have the language to process our pain and understand that it's normal to grieve and mourn the loss of our career. We know that many of our ancestors weren't given the agency to name their pain or the time to process it. I would like to build upon the frameworks of Kübler-Ross and Worden, because these ideas are important as we investigate any grief and mourning that might occur after career or job loss. Even though their frameworks are built around the concept of processing the loss of a loved one, we have to find ways to process the loss of a career too. They are both painful experiences.

Currently, you might be going through a situation in the workplace and feel isolated and alone. You might even start a line of questioning around, Why did this happen to me? What did I do to deserve this treatment? Those are questions that I used to ask myself. But I had to remind myself: I didn't create racism, and it's not my job to keep racism alive, externally or internally. I want to remind you that it's not your job either. It's a normal feeling to experience and process the loss of a career deferred. I hope you can finally stop blaming yourself for others' actions and permit yourself to shift into mourning a loss caused by systemic racism in the workplace. I would like to present to you the Four Steps of Mourning a Career:

1. Accept It
2. Process It
3. Adjust to It
4. Redefine It

Step One: Accept It

When I first left my job, as racially traumatizing as it was, I needed some time to accept it. I had to accept that I had a choice to make: to stay or go. I made the choice that centered my well-being, to go. The toxicity was already killing me softly, and I couldn't stay any longer than I already had. I had to learn to accept my final answer. Accepting what happened and why it happened was my first degree of healing. Accepting what happened to me doesn't mean I gave anyone a pass for their actions, yet I painfully understood that part of my healing ritual was not believing the lie that it was my fault that I experienced racial oppression in the workplace. There is no logical line of reasoning to dismantle a system I didn't create. I can't tell you that I was able to accept it right away; it took some time. I didn't want to accept that I had been forced out of my job by a couple of bad characters. The powers that be had personal relationships with my workplace oppressors, and they were able to dismiss my claims and feelings as though they were not facts. It was clear that my experiences didn't matter to them, and I couldn't change their minds to create a better and more inclusive place to work. That was another aspect of this situation I had to accept: I can't change a toxic workplace culture by myself, nor should I have had to. Acceptance is the first step to starting a new work life, toward packing light and being right within.

Step Two: Process It

Please keep in mind that every step you decide to embark on or consider is unique to your racialized workplace experience.

Therefore, the second step will be unique to you as well. You have to determine your definition of processing. How do you best process a situation that has occurred? How do you plan on coping with what you have recently accepted? For some of us, it's journaling, crying, or meditation. You might even decide therapy will be part of how you process the racialized event. You get to decide, but I would encourage you not to skip this step—it's critical as you continue to pack a little lighter. For me, I processed in my head, then found resources like my therapist and leaning on my faith to help me cope. I knew that I needed some time to process in private and in community. Again, processing looks different for each of us. But please remember that you are a survivor, and when that job thought you would be weak without it, you are still growing stronger.

Step 3: Adjust to It

I think adjusting to the loss I had experienced was the hardest step for me. Mainly because I had uprooted my life and made this declaration to family and friends about starting a new path, with a new job and new opportunities I thought would be better for me and my career. I had to adjust to people asking me, "How's so-and-so company treating you?" when I had already moved out of that state and started a new job. As I was going through my steps of mourning, I had to adjust to my new way of life, not tied to my former employer anymore. And I had to be okay with that, even though things didn't work out the way I planned. It happened, and I had to move on in order to heal. I had to allow myself to have the spirit of *New job, who dis?*, and be okay with that. I no longer wanted to remain emotionally connected to the racialized experiences, people, and places of my previous life.

It took time to readjust, but it was worth it. I am so glad I did, otherwise I wouldn't be writing this book for us right now. Give yourself time to readjust. Remember, you don't owe anyone anything. You don't owe people an explanation, and you don't owe them the energy of taking on their judgment. The best thing you can do is shut it all down. Any judgment you feel coming from others who don't know your story, that can't go in one of your bags. We drop bags, not pick up new ones.

Step 4: Redefine It

You might never forget how that racialized experience shook you to your core, but you don't have to be defined by it. Nikki Giovanni wrote, "Everything will change. The only question is growing up or decaying." I believe that to be true when we speak of rebirth and redefining a traumatic experience by taking control of our own narrative. For example, when some of my past racialized situations took place at work, my initial narrative in my head was, *Damn, these white people must hate me to treat me so ugly at work.* Other times, I would sit in my seat of despair and sing a Negro spiritual of my own, hummin' and praying. Once I had some healing in my life, I was able to see a once very traumatic experience with a different perspective. I learned to turn my trauma into a lesson learned and empower my future with it. Meaning that when new situations arose, I started to realize that I had the power of self-advocacy and I had my voice. In fact, I have always had my voice, I just had to decide how I wanted to use it. Through advocating for myself, I was able to see the importance of advocacy for other women of color in the workplace.

What started as a very personal journey ended with me creating a company that centers women of color in the workplace. In 2013, there was no way I could have predicted that my trauma would turn out to be an empowering portfolio of resources to make the workplace better than we found it. I hope my story can help inspire you in your future endeavors. You never know how your current or past heartbreak may help someone in the future.

The last point I will make is that I used to view my racialized pain as a loss, but now I look at that pain as a gain. It's an important part of my story. The main ingredient to being able to redefine a traumatic experience is choosing your healing. We can let a racialized experience define us, or we can choose to define it. As you continue to heal, you will be able to figure out how you want to write the remaining parts of your narrative. It doesn't have to end with a racialized experience. You have the power to decide where you take the story from here. No longer do I focus on what Kerry and my former employer did to me. I have shifted my focus on what I was able to do, despite their best efforts to uphold inequality in the workplace.

Another example of redefining a racialized moment is not centering how others might perceive my trauma. I can't control what Kerry believed her truth to be, and frankly I don't care about her version of the story. Focusing on her needs would only make me relapse. Yet, being able to redefine my tragedy and not be defined by it is powerful. You have the power to redefine your narrative, and you have the power to create a career that you don't have to suffer from. The last point I want to make about the four steps: please give yourself time to go through all of them and mourn the loss. Pretending that it didn't happen will only cause you to pick up the bags later in your career journey. We don't want any ghosts of racisms past visiting you while you are securing your seat and thriving. Part of the healing journey is to remain kind and patient with yourself. Positive vibes only!

A COMMON THREAD

Again, please don't think you are the only one going through hard times in the workplace when it comes to race. Even actress Gabrielle Union has been public about her experiences being a Black woman in the workplace. In 2019, when Union was working on *America's Got Talent*, she chose to take a stand against the inequalities she was facing and the unequal treatment of others she observed, and she was met with not having her contract renewed. Some might say, *We don't know if Union's contract wasn't renewed due to her speaking out*, and that is true. Yet, regardless of the reason, she felt the workplace didn't treat her the same because she was a Black woman. There was this narrative that she was being "difficult" and some colleagues, both Black and white, showed their lack of solidarity by claiming they had never experienced a toxic environment. They left Union to fight her battle alone. It's a story so many of us could write and coproduce: an epic tale of allies not being allies and the sisters who had to fight like their lives depend on it, now available for streaming. It's like a familiar movie that goes straight to Netflix and shows up in your recommendations section. Unfortunately, we can all be cast in our own version of this show. The thing that our allies might not understand is that racism hurts when you work at a drive-through window and racism hurts when you are a host on a popular TV show. At the end of the day, we all know the struggle to be a Black woman in the workplace, and racism sees no class, only color.

I had the pleasure of speaking at a women's conference at Salesforce, and Gabrielle Union was a speaker as well. I remember being captivated by her story, because even though my experience is different from hers, our stories had very similar themes. So much so that my eyes watered a few times, because I knew and felt the pain she spoke on. There was one comment Union made that has stuck with me years later. She referenced the care that she wished her coworkers had had for her as a Black woman in the workplace. She talked about how some of our colleagues will raise pure hell if the creamer is out or someone didn't make a fresh pot of coffee in the break room. They will tell everybody and their brother to move heaven and earth to solve that problem. But when it comes to the racism that their Black women colleagues face, they are silent as can be. They don't want to get involved. We all know that feeling too well.

The other empowering part of Union's story was that she showed what it's like to lean into your courage and push aside your caution in a public way. It takes courage to share your experiences with the world and open up the dialogue for public consumption. If we don't share our stories, then we might be blocking someone else from their healing path. I don't know if Union was thinking about that when she decided to talk about *America's Got Talent*, but I am so glad she gave voice to our struggles. Storytelling is so powerful. And as Union spoke, I felt healing taking place in me. She made a profound statement in May 2020 in an interview with *Variety*: "To experience this kind of racism at my job and there be nothing done about it, no discipline, no companywide email, no reminder of what is appropriate in the workplace?" Asking for racism to be addressed should never be considered too much. When will Black women receive fair and equal treatment and respect at work?

TAKING THE POWER BACK

I've told you the story behind how I started my company, The Memo LLC. That company probably never would have been created without the racialized trauma I experienced. I used a pain point to help spark a workplace movement that centers the careers and experiences of women of color. Not only did I start a new chapter in my career, but so many other women of color have been inspired by my journey and have taken the reins on their careers as well. They have found their voices and advocated for themselves on issues from the wage gap to promotions. They have found the courage to build their own tables. As I've said before, our healing is rarely just for us; it's also for the next generation. As we all continue to heal, we are also creating better workplaces for the next Black or Brown woman who joins us in that office or at that school. As we continue to lean into our voices and rewrite old narratives, so many more will benefit and inherit workplaces we can all be proud of.

Just for a second, think about all of the women who thought their careers were over due to a loss, yet that loss ended in them walking into their purpose. Women like Oprah. Did you know that she was fired from a television station in Baltimore, only later to become one of the most influential and powerful women in our lifetime? In an interview from 2011, she said, "Not all my memories of Baltimore are fond ones. . . . But I do have fond memories of Baltimore, because it grew me into a real woman. I came in naive, unskilled, not really knowing anything about the business—or about life. And Baltimore grew me up." I bet Oprah had no clue how that painful moment would lead her down an even better path. I know it's not easy to remind ourselves of what is possible when we are harmed, but I hope you know that healing will help you live a life worth living, inside and outside the workplace.

Please never discount how powerful it is to take a stand for yourself and ultimately for women of color in workplaces all over the country. Taking a stand for what is right won't always result in colleagues or managers finally seeing the light, understanding how racialized experiences can be traumatizing, and enacting change. Sometimes taking a stand is empowering in itself. When you take your stand in the workplace or on your healing journey, you might not be met with a gold medal or a party with lots of confetti. But you will be standing tall knowing that you are signaling to the people you work with that you won't tolerate just any ole behavior. You have boundaries. When you decide to take your stand, give yourself permission to explore what it will look like for you. It might be verbally standing up for yourself when the situation calls for it, and it might also mean not engaging in problematic conversations with someone in your office who is always looking for a racialized argument. Again, you have the power, and you get to call the shots on how you want to write your story. Just remember that every story has an author; don't let anyone else write it for you. As you take your stand, it will empower others to take theirs as well. And the image of women of color standing up from state to state is prettier than any Picasso.

There was a point in my life when I didn't see myself as radical or revolutionary or even able to take a stand. But then I realized that taking my stand was a revolutionary act. I didn't have to do it on anyone else's terms but my own. I also realized that my healing process was my own. But what I knew I couldn't keep to myself was how I learned to pack lighter when working in a world that doesn't always see me. Just like Colin Kaepernick had to take a knee, we all come to our crossroads and have to decide where we draw the line. Even though racism killed his career in 2017, Kaepernick went through his process and was able to redefine his narrative. When Kaepernick told his story, the NFL didn't get to dictate his process, even though many in the league tried. He might have ended one career, but he has inspired current and future generations to come.

These racial assaults definitely come barreling toward us like a linebacker, but we get to decide how we stand guard and run offense. We have experienced our trauma, but we aren't defined by it. As we continue to share our stories one by one, women around the globe will know that we stand in solidarity to fight racist systems. We make progress by telling our own stories, so that no one can twist the narrative to exploit our racialized pain or minimize our stories to their lowest common denominator. Our storytelling holds them accountable.

Time to Unpack and Reassess

1. Have you ever felt like you were the only one going through a racialized experience in the workplace?
2. How does hearing the stories of others inspire your healing journey?
3. In this chapter, I mentioned racism killing careers. Have you experienced this and what year did this racialized event occur?
4. Which of the Four Steps of Mourning a Career do you find to be the most challenging and why?
5. Please finish this statement: I am not my trauma. I am able to turn my trauma into _____, and I will be reborn and redefine _____ as I continue my journey toward healing from racial trauma.

Chapter 9

TAKE CARE

Dealing with a heart that I didn't break
—Drake, "Take Care"

Y ou've made it to the end of *Right Within*, and I hope you feel like you can pack a little lighter in the workplace. How are you feeling? Hopefully you feel a sense of peace and optimism knowing that you aren't alone on your healing journey. I hope you feel like you owe it to yourself to go the distance. Because what we know to be true is that if we don't prioritize our emotional health and rid ourselves of the racial trauma that has tried to hold us back, no one else will. And if at first you don't succeed, I hope you will try again and again. You are worth the journey, and you are worth the inner and outer work. Many Buddhists believe that we are the most powerful healer of our problems. Even though I am not a Buddhist, I believe we possess the ability to move our lives in a direction that no longer weighs us down with our racialized workplace trauma.

PACK LIGHT

Maybe you've been healing while reading or listening to this book, or perhaps you are on the verge of realizing that if you don't try, like Brandy said, "almost doesn't count." That's not to say that if you don't completely heal in this lifetime you failed. I just hope you will try out a few healing tools and see where they take you, and I hope you will acknowledge that the process of healing could be beneficial to you. Because without healing, your bags of trauma will get heavier and you might need not just a therapist but a chiropractor too. Come on girl, let 'em go. Let those bags go! I think you will feel better knowing that you created a treatment plan that allowed yourself to live a fuller life on this side of the planet.

When we started our journey together, I asked if you would consider exploring what healing could look like for you. I realize that, when I asked you this, you may or may not have been in a space to fully understand what that journey might look like. Even having read the book, you still might be uncertain, and that's fine too. It would be insensitive of me if I didn't address that while going through each chapter, you might have been reminded of some very painful workplace situations from your own past. I remember how I started questioning myself during my early days in corporate America, and I took that shame and carried it with me for many years. Looking back now, I realize that was a bag I shouldn't have ever picked up. All too often, the fault is in the environment. It was never created with us at the center. And that is why we must work to dismantle discrimination in these exclusionary spaces every day.

Dismantling oppressive systems can be hard. In this book, I have recounted stories from one of the jobs where I was a consultant, early in my career. After our training academy, everyone was being deployed to their various client locations. The HR office requested that all the on-site consultants purchase their flight and hotel accommodations, and we would later get reimbursed for our expenses. You are probably thinking, *Okay, that sounds like a reasonable standard procedure, right?* The only issue was that I didn't have a credit card or a savings account that I could tap into to front the money. The rest of my cohort had personal credit cards or families that could help them, and no one seemed pressed like I did. I felt so ashamed and embarrassed that I didn't have a credit card. And, prior to starting this new role, I barely had enough money to make ends meet. I didn't have the language for how I was feeling then, but now some would call it imposter syndrome. I felt the imposter-syndrome monster growing inside of my mind, bigger and bigger by the minute. I was at a loss. I didn't have the money to pay for my temporary move. Why would they just assume that everybody has access to the same resources? Because everyone in charge is operating from a place of privilege. Must be nice!

You might be asking yourself, *Why didn't you have a credit card, Minda?* To be honest, I was used to paying my bills and expenses with cash, my ATM card, or a check. I never applied for a credit card in college because I didn't want to have a bunch of debt outside of my student loans. I had no financial guidance at this stage of my life, and I thought I was doing the right thing. I didn't know what I didn't know. Unfortunately, my company did not take into account that not everyone has the means to simply be reimbursed, and now I felt like the odd man out. I spent the next twenty-four hours wanting to pull my hair out and beat myself up for not having what everyone else had. There was no way I was going to get a credit card in a week, especially since I didn't have established credit. The money my company needed me to have was in the thousands, not just a couple hundred dollars. My stomach was in knots, because the next day I knew I would have to walk into the HR office and admit that I wasn't who they thought I was.

WHO AM I?

Let me back up a bit. When I took this job, I was leaving my former workplace where I was being underpaid. I had just enough money to pay my monthly bills and a few dollars here and there for the things that brought me joy. When I got hired, I fondly remember my parents taking me to Marshalls and helping me buy some new suits. I was so happy purchasing my first Tahari skirt suit, which I found on the clearance rack. They bought me about five suits, and I was ready for the world. Couldn't nobody tell me I wasn't so fresh and so clean. When I walked into my first day of consultancy boot camp, I was the dopest person in the room. Not to mention, I bought a nice new wig—nothing like a new hair piece! I felt good about myself. I remember feeling like they would take me seriously because I was dressed the part. I had done all the code-switching I could do, and by the end of our cohort training, I had become one of the company's "rising stars." And now their rising star had to go and tell them, *I ain't got it like that. Don't let these clearance suits and "proper" talk fool you.* I had tricked myself into believing I belonged, until I didn't—or so I thought.

I cannot explain to you the shame I felt. It was deep. Have you ever experienced a similar situation? Perhaps you felt shame at first but, looking back, you can see that the situation was all on them, and that you had no reason to feel that way. Often, we don't initially see it that way and so we add that unnecessary trauma into our bags. I took on racialized trauma that I never should have been asked to carry in the first place. Back then, I felt like I had no choice but to show my hand. I felt like it was my fault I didn't have the resources I needed. And I felt like it was my fault that I didn't come from a background where I could just call somebody I knew and ask them for a couple-thousand-dollar advance. I ended up carrying that shame to every city thereafter. I allowed the shame to weigh me down.

I mustered some courage and went to have the conversation that I dreaded. I wish I could tell you that it went great and that I was stressed out for nothing. But the HR department made a big deal about it, and before I knew it everyone in the office knew that I didn't have a credit card or money to front-load my expenses. My cohort found out, and every senior leader now looked at me like, *You poor little Black girl.* Or so it felt. Maybe I am projecting a bit. I am sure some of those were my own issues. Long story short, a bunch of people got involved and the company ended up giving me a moving allowance. Which in reality they should have done at the freaking start. But they weren't inclusive and had not considered that every staff member doesn't have the same resources and education around certain topics. That entire week became a showdown of the haves and have-nots. I felt like a charity case by the end of it.

At that time in my career, it felt like being Black was a burden while working in white spaces. With healing, I was able to learn to love myself again. I was able to dismantle the debilitating thoughts and replace them with positive affirmations. I learned to remind myself that I was "proud to be Black like me," as the country singer Mickey Guyton says. All of that shame I felt about not having a large amount of money—most Americans probably don't have that money either, and it should never even have entered the equation. An equitable environment means that everyone has the resources they need to do the job, and if you don't, then the employer needs to get with the program. Don't for a minute let all of the trauma we've experienced in the workplace have you questioning your place in this world. Those causing the harm are the ones who don't belong.

So let's heal and learn to pack a little lighter, because imposter syndrome can no longer take up space in our lives. Time's up! Oh, and you know what else ain't nobody got time for? Trying to rationalize a toxic environment. I told myself a story that had me at the center with a deficit. When in reality, my former employer was the one who was morally bankrupt. They were excluding talent by not accommodating their employees. It makes me wonder how many other employers are doing the same thing.

Before I move on, I feel the need to unpack this piece of the trauma just a bit further. It took me so long to finally heal from feeling like I wasn't enough. This was the same company where my manager racialized my orange nail polish. This is also the same company where I had the experience with Danny, who tried to sabotage me to get ahead. I was met with racialized trauma every day, forty-plus hours a week. Many of my early career moments as the only Black woman in the workplace resulted in racialized abuse on various levels from many different colleagues at the same company. It took a lot of time to unpack that I didn't deserve that treatment and that it wasn't my fault. It wasn't until a decade later that I finally started to examine where this trauma had latched onto me.

Now I know that I wasn't the problem. It was clearly a toxic work environment. And the toxicity was being enabled by the leaders who allowed it and participated in the harm. No one was ever held accountable or forced to see how they were the problem. Additionally, my former employer should have had a travel policy in place to accommodate consultants who liked to use their own cards and those who didn't. I shouldn't have been made to feel less than because I didn't have a credit card at that time in my life. I was their so-called rising star; they should have made sure I had the resources to advance in my career, not question whether I needed them.

I believe this is a huge issue with systemic racism in the workplace. People will try to make you feel like you are the problem or a failure. And as you are experiencing feeling othered or singled out, it becomes easier and easier to feel the infamous imposter syndrome. No wonder I carried imposter syndrome in my bag for so many years. With all of the experiences I had, any sane person would start to question themself. As we begin to heal, we will start to realize how many of our companies, organizations, and colleagues have failed us. We aren't failures or less than. And the imposter syndrome that many of us have picked up in our careers and carried around with us no longer serves us, and it never has. My prayer is that we never pick it up ever again.

I tell you this story because I didn't realize how that moment in my early twenties had stayed with me, even though I desperately wanted to forget it. Unfortunately, we experience so many racialized situations in the workplace that it would be too much to recount all of them. But there are some that form us as the women we are and shape the way we navigate the workplace, for better or worse. It was that situation that made me start to feel like I wasn't enough. Perhaps on the outside it might not have looked that way because I appeared to be "so put together," as many of my white colleagues would tell me. But internally I felt like I had to prove that I wasn't really the girl who didn't have the money to cover her expenses up front. (I actually think that's a lot to expect of a twentysomething in the first place, and I wish I had known about this when I was hired, as I could have made some provisions, but I digress.)

The moral of the story is that it was a bag that I picked up early in my career and it wasn't until writing this book that I finally realized I had never truly put it down. Now I am working to pack lighter and be right within, right along with you. I hope you don't forget that healing is a daily practice, but you don't have to heal alone. Healing takes work for all of us who want to do it. And now you have the tools to keep on keeping on.

CHEERS TO YOU

I am excited to hear what new healing tools you might decide to use, and I hope you will start to feel lighter as time goes on. Hell, I hope you feel a little lighter right now. Healing starts with acknowledging that we are experiencing pain or have experienced racial trauma. And if you are able to articulate that, then you are already on your way. Oh, and I want to remind you that your healing journey doesn't have to be delayed until you get the right manager. Your healing journey doesn't have to start next year when you get a new job. Your healing can start right now. If you don't believe me, remember the lines from the Drake song "Take Care": "When you're ready, just say you're ready." His song is on point because it's about taking care. I hope that you will continue to take care and be kind to yourself. Because this cold work world won't do it for you.

As women of color, our mental wellness and health have to be on our agenda, on our vision boards, and in our prayers if we want to thrive at the table. Take it from me. I am so happy that I invested in myself and decided to put in the work to put myself first. I knew I deserved to heal, not just for me but to help save the next generation from a continued legacy of racial trauma. I wrote this book just for you. I couldn't go another day knowing that so many of us will be racially insulted and assaulted and feel as though this is just the way it is. Racial trauma in the workplace doesn't have to be the norm, and change starts internally. It starts with us activating our power and using our tools when we need them. As you use your healing tools, please continue reflecting on some of the questions that you answered at the end of each chapter. Our healing is in our hands, and we can hold ourselves accountable to stay the course.

Now that we are at the end of this, I can't finish without asking you: What does healing mean to you now? I am curious to see if your definition has changed over the course of this book. And I am excited to hear from you on how you have grown and what concepts resonated most. As I've always said, I don't have all the answers, but I wanted to share some tools with you to add to your career and healing tool kit so you can secure your seat at whatever table is best for you. I wanted to be sure you could proceed with less racial baggage than you started with.

This chapter is intended to serve as an additional resource. Please add me to your healing advisory squad for those moments when you want to run around the building and scream. Use me as a healing advisor when you have taken a big step forward and you are celebrating the release of what no longer holds you back. I definitely want to hear how your healing is coming along. I will be here for it all. But in the meantime, I want you to use these resources and share them with others who could benefit from packing lighter too. We need the collective to heal so we can bring to work the authentic pieces of ourselves that matter most.

Although you've been doing all of your internal work to dismantle the racist forces that have tried to harm your career, I couldn't end this book without addressing the leaders and managers within companies and organizations. I included what I call a Letter to Management in the appendix. Even though this book centers on the experiences of racialized trauma that women of color face, much of that trauma is a product of the leadership and management within our places of employment. These racialized experiences are often inflicted by the people who call themselves our managers, and often these managers are white people without extensive training on how to support a diverse staff. I would be doing you and me a disservice if I didn't speak directly to them in this book as well. I told you, healing takes work, and I am going to use my healing tools and speak to the issues head-on. Please allow me to do the heavy lifting. You deserve a champion.

ACCOUNTABILITY

We must hold our current and future managers accountable for driving talented people like ourselves out of jobs and careers. If you are a manager, including a white manager, please visit **www.beingrightwithin.com** and you will find a Manager's Pledge and other resources I created to equip managers to better support women of color in a workplace that was not designed with diversity in mind. I believe the future of work will require emotionally intelligent managers who can lead through the lens of diversity, inclusion, equity, and belonging. As a reader, please provide your company and organization with this book and share these resources for racial justice so you can have healing and maintenance tools in the places where you spend a large part of your time.

According to the 2020 *The State of Black Women in Corporate America* report from Lean In, Black women are experiencing the worst of what the workplace has to offer. Yes, women in general experience oppression, but let's not forget that there is a hierarchy of oppression and white women tend to face less opposition than other groups of women. The report shows that "49% of Black women feel that their race or ethnicity will make it harder for them to get a raise, promotion, or chance to get ahead, compared to just 3% of white women and 11% of women overall." What this statistic says to me is that industries need to do a lot of work to invest in Black women and women of color. These are not just stories that we've made up in our minds; these are our lived experiences. Some folks might not value our feelings, but those numbers don't lie. The silver lining to these sad statistics is that there are many opportunities to do right by Black and Brown women in the workplace.

Now, returning to my Black and Brown readers: Before you dive into the additional healing resources that I've provided for you, I have two more requests. First, please consider taking the Healing Pledge at **www.beingrightwithin.com**. I created this site as a community-building tool for everyone who reads or listens to this book. I created the website so we can connect with each other and serve as healing advisors and champions for each other on our healing journey. I believe that healing in community is important, and my commitment to making the workplace better than I found it doesn't stop just because you are at the end of the book. I am rooting for your continued success both internally and externally. But what really matters most to me is that you fight those workplace demons that have tried to take the best years of your life. You take them back and own the rest of your journey. You got it, girl, you got it!

Now that you are on the road to healing, I hope that you will hold yourself accountable for doing the best you can to continue healing and growing through those experiences that have tried to stunt your growth. If need be, rely on your advisors and champions to help you stay committed to the journey. As I mentioned, you can find the Healing Pledge at **www.beingrightwithin.com**, but I have included the pledge and other resources below as well. This pledge signifies that we are packing lighter and that racial trauma no longer has a place in our lives. I think we can agree that all racial trauma has done is take precious time away from our ability to thrive, in and out of the workplace. And, just so you know, I am taking this pledge as well.

On the website, you can download a special badge to share on your social media pages with others who might need to consider healing from their racialized workplace trauma. By posting your badge, you are communicating that healing is required for longevity of peace, and sometimes people just need to see others taking action to activate their next steps. Please continue to affirm yourself, love yourself, and be kind to yourself—I cannot say that enough.

We don't have to be bound by our racialized past. Let us always remind ourselves that the dominant narratives that are negatively created about us are not our bags to carry. Let them keep their own bags. We have the opportunity to decide right now to change our way of thinking and rewrite the story of how workplace racialized experiences tried to take us out, but we persisted. I have complete faith in you that you can and will decide to be right within and pack light.

The Healing Pledge

I, <u>insert your name</u>, pledge that I will no longer be held captive to past or current racialized trauma in the workplace. I honor myself, and I will continue to create healthy boundaries that center my overall career health. I commit to packing lighter and experiencing career success on my own terms. I realize any microaggressions, macroaggressions, biases, or prejudices that have tried to hold me back from being able to thrive in the workplace can no longer stunt my mental health and career. I will do my best to continue to allow myself to heal and use the various healing tools available to me because healing is not a one-time event, but a lifestyle. I commit to practicing healing every day. My healing matters.

_____

Below you will find various healing tools and resources to add to your healing tool kit. I don't believe in sending you off without a parting gift. I have included resources I have used myself and those recommended by others. As I've said before, success is not a solo sport, and you might need a squad of people in the community to help you stay the course. Your ability to continue to heal is your choice, and I hope you will always choose you. Because all you need in this life is yourself and your healing.

Churches and Faith-Based Counseling Centers

- **Bishop Vashti Murphy McKenzie**
  www.vashtimckenzie.com
- **Champion Counseling Center at Faithful Central Bible Church**, located in Inglewood, California
  www.faithfulcentral.com
- **City of God Church**, located in Rock Falls, Illinois
  http://cityofgodsterling.org
- **The HOPE Center at First Corinthian Baptist Church**, located in New York, New York
  https://fcbcnyc.org/care/hopecentermentalhealth

Therapy Directory

- **BEAM** is a collective of advocates, yoga teachers, artists, therapists, lawyers, religious leaders, teachers, psychologists, and activists committed to the emotional and mental health and healing of Black communities.
  https://wellness.beam.community/
- **National Queer and Trans Therapists of Color Network** is a healing justice organization committed to transforming mental health for queer and trans people of color.
  www.nqttcn.com/directory
- **Therapy for Black Girls** is an online space dedicated to encouraging the mental wellness of Black women and girls.
  https://providers.therapyforblackgirls.com/

Podcasts

- *Heal Sh*t Podcast* is hosted by Tiffany Ellis and Shanta Jackson. This podcast normalizes therapy for millennial women in minority communities.
  https://podsandpr.com/
- *The Homecoming Podcast* is hosted by Dr. Thema Bryant-Davis. This podcast can facilitate your journey home to yourself by providing weekly inspiration and health tips.
  www.drthema.com/
- *Therapy for Black Girls Podcast* is hosted by Dr. Joy Harden Bradford. This podcast is an online space dedicated to encouraging the mental wellness of Black women and girls.
  https://therapyforblackgirls.com/podcast/

Books

- *The Inner Work of Racial Justice: Healing Ourselves and Transforming Our Communities Through Mindfulness* by Rhonda V. Magee
- *My Grandmother's Hands: Racialized Trauma and the Pathway to Mending Our Hearts and Bodies* by Resmaa Menakem
- *Post Traumatic Slave Syndrome: America's Legacy of Enduring Injury and Healing* by Dr. Joy DeGruy
- *The Racial Healing Handbook: Practical Activities to Help You Challenge Privilege, Confront Systemic*

Racism, and Engage in Collective Healing by Anneliese A. Singh
- *A Sisters Siesta* by Jasmin Forts

Online and Offline Communities

- **Ethel's Club** creates healing spaces that center and celebrate people of color through conversation, wellness, and creativity.
  www.ethelsclub.com
- **HealHaus** is a community that is dedicated to changing the stigma attached to healing.
  www.healhaus.com
- **Refresh with Ekene** is a community of mentorship and coaching for high-achieving and spiritual women.
  www.refreshforlife.com
- **Sad Girls Club** is committed to showing up for Black women and people of color, creating community, and providing resources to better your mental health.
  www.instagram.com/sadgirlsclub
- **Sista Afya** is a mental wellness community that provides monthly support groups, group therapy sessions, and workshops for Gen Z and millennial Black women.
  www.sistaafya.com

Our time together might have come to an end with this book, yet our healing journey is just getting started. For so many years, I didn't even know that healing from racial trauma in the workplace was an option. And I would imagine that many of you might have thought the same thing. I am excited that the women of color coming behind us will learn they can heal much earlier in their careers. Hopefully, because we are taking a stand now, our workplaces will change to the point where the next generation won't have to experience racialized workplace trauma in the first place. Because there is no room for it in our futures.

I have tried my best to be as honest as I could with you as I wrote *Right Within*. I shared my stories and the healing tools that helped and continue to help me heal. The scariest part for me initially was sharing my story out loud. When I realized that I had a lot of healing to do due to the racialized trauma I had experienced, I feared what others might say. Fear was probably the most paralyzing thing I faced during my healing process. I had spent so much of my adult working career walking on eggshells and catering to white people, who were the vast majority within the spaces where I worked. I only knew to be fearful. Our former first lady Mrs. Michelle Obama put it this way: "You can't make decisions based on fear and the possibility of what might happen." And that is when I really began to understand that fear couldn't go where I was headed and healing superseded any fear of the unknown, because I knew so many more women of color would benefit when I stopped being scared.

I didn't even realize that I was never centering myself. I was still trying to center those who oppressed me. It can be painful to uncover all of the damage that racially abusive workplaces have caused. It was initially hard for me to heal because, like Lauryn Hill said, "baby girl, respect is just a minimum . . . you still defending 'em." When you are traumatized, you will try to find some good in the people who harmed you the most. I could no longer defend folks. I had to finally realize that I had to protect myself, and I deserve that.

My hope for you is that you won't wake up each morning dreading getting ready for work because you know you will be met with a racialized and toxic environment. My hope is that you will use your healing tools and find the workplaces that work for you, speak up when you need to, and walk away when you decide it's time. I hope you will feel encouraged that you won't be healing alone. There are so many more women of color who will be healing right along with you. Additionally, my hope is that our employers will do the work they need to do to dismantle racially toxic workplaces, because it's not our job to fix those. We will be working on our healing, because it's time we finally center ourselves—that is how we will be right within.

ACKNOWLEDGMENTS

Thank you, God, for taking me on this healing path. I originally thought this journey was just for me, but now I know it was much bigger. To my Team Harts, family members, my chosen family, and friends: this life is so much sweeter with you by my side. To Miranda, you helped unleash the thinker and advocate I am today, and I am forever grateful. To my mentors and success partners, thank you for always believing in me. To my first therapist and all of the faith leaders who have helped me on this journey, you are the real ones. To Emi and Monica, to everyone at Seal Press, you believed in my voice and our mission, and you are my book dream team. To the media, companies, and organizations that have supported my work, success is not a solo sport. I also want to extend a special thank-you to my on- and offline squad who rock with me. I could not do this without you. God bless, and never be afraid to heal. And to Boston, mommy loves you. xoxo

Appendix

TO LEADERS AND MANAGERS

My hope is that you will continue to lean into your courage, educate yourself, and read *Right Within*. When I wrote my first book, *The Memo*, I interviewed over one hundred women of color. Over 70 percent of them stated that they felt like their managers were not invested in their success. Earlier I mentioned *The State of Black Women in Corporate America* report, and there are some inexcusable and downright offensive statistics when it comes to the advancement of Black women in the workplace. In the 2020 report, Black women held 1.6 percent of vice president roles and 1.4 percent of executive suite positions.

To give you just a little more context, "more than 590 companies employing more than 22 million people, along with a quarter of a million individual employees, have participated in [the] Women in the Workplace" study on which the report was based. So I don't want you thinking these stats are isolated situations; there are common issues taking place across many companies.

The report shows that Black women receive less support and advocacy from their managers compared to the white women who were interviewed. Unfortunately, when a woman of color doesn't have a manager who is supporting and advocating for her, then the manager is denying the employee the opportunity to perform at her highest level and showcase her best work. Without manager support, women of color often aren't thought of for stretch assignments, and are denied opportunities for growth. Managers could do more to advocate for employees of color by noticing if they are being socially isolated and working to help them navigate office politics.

I am by no means saying that all managers are displaying this lack of professional investment as it pertains to Black women, but these stats lead me to believe that not enough managers are creating an equal playing field. I believe that lack of managerial support is directly correlated with these low percentages of women of color, and Black women in particular, in leadership roles. Black and Brown women are often not being retained and advanced in corporate America at the same rate as our white counterparts. Now, let me repeat it again: I am not suggesting that you are one of those managers, but if there seems to be few people of color in senior roles in your industry, please consider how you may have played a part in the lack of investment in women of color. What could better look like if you were fully invested in everyone on your team? Because women of color cannot promote themselves. They need a success partner and champion as they continue to climb the ladder. And if Black women in particular are aware of these statistics and experience this ambivalent treatment from their managers, what type of psychological safety do you think it provides them? The answer is it doesn't; it just perpetuates a system of racism. But don't hate the player—you gotta hate the game you're playing!

When I was in corporate America, I had a couple of white men who used their privilege to help me advance in my career. One of my champions was Charles. Charles was probably thirty-plus years older than me. We both were in the philanthropic profession and met at an annual gala, serendipitously sitting at the same table. I think it was one of those tables where they put everyone who came alone to make them feel less lonely, but it was hella awkward. I never would have imagined that making small talk with Charles would end up changing my career for the better. That evening, Charles gave me his business card and I chose to do something different—I actually followed up with him via email. He had a very successful career in our field, and I was currently trying to make a name for myself. Over time, he extended his social capital and helped make introductions for me. There were times he reviewed my résumé to make sure I was putting my best foot forward and telling my career story in a compelling way. And he helped me on various occasions navigate promotions, hard conversations, and salary negotiations.

Charles didn't owe me anything, but as we built a relationship, he was invested in my success. Let's be honest, managers tend to invest their time and energy into the people on their team they identify with, and often those are people who look like them or have similar backgrounds. Me and Charles couldn't have been more different. We were odder than the odd couple themselves. Charles didn't help me advance my career because I reminded him of his daughter. And he didn't choose to help me because I played golf with him and the guys. Charles removed any bias he might have had and allowed himself to use his social capital and share it with me. We both had fundraising in common and were in an industry we both enjoyed; we bonded over philanthropy. He didn't have to do it, oh, but I am glad he did. Every woman of color needs her Charles. And having someone like Charles can come in various forms. My question to you is, who will you be a Charles to? Being a success partner to a woman of color on your team or in your department will require you to build a relationship with her. We can't be the only ones working toward building sustainable and authentic workplace relationships.

Let me explain something. You sit in a unique position. You have the ability to grow, enhance, or stunt a person's career. I don't mean any disrespect by that, but the truth is the truth. As part of the management team, you hold a level of influence within your company or organization. You have the ability to be a partner on the road to success for a woman of color in the workplace. I have clear receipts of how Charles helped me. And he didn't help me in word only; he took action. You have to be the action verb. Being a champion will require you to help dismantle dysfunctional past systems and create new systems that don't oppress women of color in the workplace. For example, if you have someone on your team who is clearly causing racialized toxicity, choosing to ignore that person's behavior, tone, or language is not an option. It's up to you to set a healthy tone for the team's interpersonal behavior. That might require creating norms and articulating which behaviors won't be tolerated. Don't forfeit the team's development by never calling out those who are oppressing people on your team. And don't allow the oppressors to play the victim while bullying others.

I wish that I had had managers in my former life who championed an inclusive work environment. I can honestly say, over my fifteen-year career I never experienced a manager who set the tone for equity and psychological safety. There was always some form of racialized bias that constantly went unchecked. When you're the only or one of few on your team, this kind of environment is extremely isolating and demeaning. If you are not comfortable with managing a diverse team and holding all team members accountable, then you might consider being an individual contributor instead of a manager. Not everyone is meant to manage, and you have to decide if it's fair to lead a team if you aren't equipped to do so. It's unfair to the women who are not valued by their managers. Too many women of color are choosing to leave corporate America, not because they want to work for themselves, but because of who they work for. I am sure you don't want to purposely harm someone on your team, and if that's true, you will require accountability and tools to help you lead with equity.

I created the Manager's Pledge, and I hope you will consider signing it. I hope you will consider helping dismantle a toxic racial culture inside the workplace. And I hope that you are dedicated to the success of every person on your team. The pledge also asks you to take one step further by asking your company or organization for resources to ensure that you are able to properly lead and invest in everyone on your team. It's imperative that you help create an environment where women of color can come to you with racialized experiences and you will hear them out by practicing courageous listening. Remember, even if you don't see the incident or you have a relationship with someone who is causing harm, you still have to be an inclusive manager at all times. Being a courageous listener will require you to provide empathy, dignity, and respect. In other words, you will pledge to hear women of color out.

What I am telling you might be hard to hear or read, but these are the facts. Perhaps you are thinking, *What does she know?* or *I am doing the best I can.* I'm saying that, whatever the baseline, you could always be growing as a manager and doing better. Each one of us has biases, and creating a work culture in which everyone on the team feels seen, heard, and valued takes a lot of courage and practice. Creating an inclusive culture is not a one-time conversation or event. It's my job and purpose to make sure I leave the workplace better than I found it; I can't do that without addressing the role managers play in the advancement of women of color. I hope you will always be curious in your pursuit to figure out what better looks like. No one is doing it perfectly, so there will always be room to grow. But it's hard to grow when your education is not cultivated and your actions are never held at a best-in-class standard. We shouldn't hold managers to a low level of accountability. Inclusive culture starts from the top down.

Also, please don't think I am only here to serve as your drill sergeant. I am here as your champion as well. Often, I reference a book of leadership quotes by motivational speaker Clifton Anderson called *A Year Wiser*. In this book is a quote by a man named Darren Washington, and it says, "The sum of a man's life is the difference he's made in the lives of others." As a manager or leader within your organization, you have the ability to change lives and inspire those you lead. You have to ask yourself how you will contribute to leaving a legacy that didn't oppress women of color in the workplace. You also have to ask how you will contribute to ensuring that Black and Brown careers matter. Only you can answer those questions, but I hope you allow yourself time to figure out what the answers are and take action. Take action by listening to women of color, educating yourself on women of color, and activating your partnership to advance and not harm their careers.

Lastly, if you go to **www.beingrightwithin.com**, I have provided some resources for managers and leaders, because success is not a solo sport. In order to change the way systemic racism has affected many women of color, we will need you to put in the work by unlearning what has been comfortable. Your management activism will be required in the future of work. The acknowledgment of a woman's talent often rides on how effective her managers are. The role of a manager is to help provide psychological safety for all of their employees, not just some. Many companies and organizations have failed women of color, and you can chart a new course of action today. Start with leaning into your courage and pushing aside your caution, because no woman of color will benefit if you remain cautious and keep the workplace working for just some and not all.

Okay, I lied. I am not done just yet. I have to address one more issue: if you are a manager who is from a marginalized community, please don't participate in systemic or internal racism by not advancing people on your team who look like you or by avoiding hiring people who you identify with racially. I have consulted for many companies, and I have heard too many stories of people of color not hiring or advancing other people of color because their colleagues might think they are only doing so because they are Black or Brown. We cannot participate in bias, and this type of bias is just as insidious as any other form. I implore you not to perpetuate racist systems of oppression. Being a better manager isn't reserved for white people only. We need an all-hands-on-deck effort when it comes to the advancement and safety of women of color in the workplace.

THE MANAGER'S PLEDGE

- I will acknowledge that I have biases that I need to understand and reconcile.
- I will commit to engaging in courageous conversations. They might sometimes be difficult, but I know they are necessary to create an inclusive workplace.

- I will challenge myself to hold other colleagues accountable when I have heard or observed racialized tones, behaviors, and actions.
- I will learn to humanize the experiences of all my colleagues and seek to understand and listen to their perspectives and lived experiences, particularly when they differ from my own.
- I will share my experiences and educational journey to help other managers create restorative justice practices.
- Even if I make a mistake, I commit to the daily practice of being a better manager who is committed to equity for all.

For more information, please visit **www.beingrightwithin .com** and **www.wocequity.com** to help create racial equity for women of color. The Women of Color Equity Initiative is a resource I created in 2018 to increase the number of Black women and other women of color in management and executive roles via our sourcing database.

INDEX

Minda Harts is the CEO of The Memo LLC, a career development platform for women of color; a professor of public service at NYU; and the author of *The Memo*. She was named a LinkedIn Top Voice for Equity in the Workplace and was honored as one of BET's Future 40. She speaks at Fortune 500 companies and hosts the podcast *Secure the Seat*. She lives in New York City.